BATTERED WOMEN

BATTERED WOMEN

Living With the Enemy

by Anna Kosof

Women Then — Women Now

Franklin Watts
New York Chicago London Toronto Sydney

Library of Congress Cataloging-in-Publication Data

Kosof, Anna.
Battered women: living with the enemy / by Anna Kosof.
    p.   cm — (Women then—women now)
Includes bibliographical references and index.
ISBN 0-531-11203-9 (lib. bdg.)
1. Abused women—United States—Juvenile literature. 2. Abused women—
Services for—United States—Juvenile literature.
[1. Abused women.] I. Title. II. Series.
HV6626.2.K67 1994
362.82'92'0973—dc20   94-29529 CIP AC

First paperback edition published in 1995 by Franklin Watts
ISBN 0-531-15755-5

CONTENTS

CHAPTER ONE
AN EPIDEMIC

Domestic violence is the most widespread form of violence in the United States and is the major cause of injury to women. The Federal Bureau of Investigation (FBI) receives reports of a woman being beaten every fifteen seconds.[1]

According to the first major study of battered women, conducted in 1976, women experienced physical assault in nearly one third of all American families. Every year, an estimated three to four million women in the United States are beaten in their homes by their husbands, ex–husbands, or male lovers. Twenty percent of hospital emergency visits by women are due to battering. According to the Centers for Disease Control and Prevention in Atlanta, a woman is in nine times greater danger of being the victim of a violent act in her own home than on the streets.[2] More than 50 percent of all women killed in the U.S. are killed by their male partner. This silent epidemic occurs in all socioeconomic, ethnic, cultural, racial and religious groups. If these statistics are frightening, so too is the life of the woman who has been battered.

Like rape, the crime of domestic violence is underreported. Data is difficult to obtain because the crime usually occurs at night, at home, and with no witnesses. Women often are in isolation when it comes to family violence, for there is a deep-seated sense of shame associated with this crime.

Family violence has deep roots in our history. For many centuries and in many cultures, the male head of a family was allowed — by custom and sometimes by law — to use violence against his wife and children. They were considered his property. The everyday expression "rule of thumb" comes from an old English legal doctrine: a man could beat his wife with a stick, as long as the stick was no thicker than his thumb.

Today, many people still believe that family violence is a private concern of the family, not a matter for law and government, and not a crime. After all, they reason, isn't a man's home his castle? The men who batter their partners claim that they have a right to do this, and no government should have the ability to interfere.

Neither domestic violence nor the death of perhaps 4,000 women annually seems comprehensible without exploring the myths that surround this issue.[3] We need to gain a clear picture of how this problem can occur so frequently and put millions of lives in danger. We need to explore who the victims are, and how they got into such an abusive situation. What can permit three to four million women to be beaten in their homes each year by the men who claim to love them: their husbands, their partners, their lovers?

In this book, we will hear the stories of abused women. We will try to understand the cycle of violence and the men and the women who live these tragic lives. We will also look at why the courts have offered little protection to these women, why many women are afraid to call the police, and what happens to many women when they do call for help.

We will try to separate fact from fiction in order to understand and, eventually, to prevent these tragic occurrences. Unfortunately, while we may not always know it, some of these victims are people we know and love.

CHAPTER TWO

THE MYTHS

Domestic violence is often dismissed as a problem that affects only a small group of women. As the facts show, this problem is not rare. Many experts believe this problem to be an epidemic. But as long as society believes the myth — that the problem affects only a few isolated women — it is hard to respond with legislation or protection for the abused, or treat family violence as the epidemic that it is.

A second myth is that this violence takes place only far away from our homes, or our friends' homes, or our neighborhood. This also is not true. If violence doesn't occur in your home, it occurs very close to you — in your apartment building, on your street, and to someone you know.

The third myth is that middle class and affluent women are not battered. According to researchers, however, family violence affects all classes, reaching into middle- and upper-class communities where the women may be reluctant to reveal their beatings for fear of social embarrassment, or harm to their own or their husband's career, or injury to their children. Most of the statistics on domestic violence come from studies of lower economic class families, because these families are more accessible to government researchers. Low income women come in contact regularly with government and community agencies, so their problems are more visible. These women live in more densely populated areas, such as the housing projects where their screams are more readily overheard. They come in contact with social workers or welfare workers so their black and blue marks are more often noticed.

A fourth myth is that women from some ethnic backgrounds are not battered. Studies show that women of all cultures and races (Anglo women as well as Latinos, Asians, African Americans, European Americans) are beaten, and in many cases, seriously enough to warrant emergency visits to the hospital. Recent immigrants may be more reluctant to call the police and to report abuse. This only underscores the fact that this crime is vastly underreported. So, another myth is shattered.

Fifth, it is commonly believed that the abused women cannot leave their homes because they lack the resources to do so; they are uneducated and without skills. But many battered women are employed outside the home and are educated.

Another common myth is that the women stay because they like being beaten and abused. In fact, women do not leave the abuser because it is very difficult to escape.[1] It is a mistake to believe that if women want to leave, they can easily get protection from the police. Even after years of trying, often at great risk, to leave the relationship, women have found that they receive very little support from the police system. The women who were interviewed found that not only were the police ineffective in shielding them, but in many cases turning to the police made things at home much worse.

There are many more "myths" that are believed by the general public and the women themselves. The myth that the women provoke the men, that they "deserve" to be hit and beaten, that they are responsible for pushing the abuser past his breaking point, is one misconception that we need to explore and then quickly dismiss. This assumes that men need not take responsibility for their own actions, an assumption that is false and dangerous. Men, as well as women, are responsible for their own actions. The idea that the blame can be placed on the victim compounds the abuse and causes both physical and psychological pain. The "blaming the victim" concept is one that many of the women had been brainwashed into accepting.

Why don't the women just get out? Many people wonder why they stay in a dangerous situation. It is, unfortunately, a myth to believe that the women can always leave home. Many cannot leave; and many of them know that if they try to leave, they may be killed. Sadly, statistics bear out this fear. Seventy-five percent of abused women have been killed, when they attempted to leave or after they left home.[2] It is hard to imagine the danger that they face, the domination that the men exercise over them, and the violence and fear that traumatizes the family. The psychological inability to stand up to the men, the women's low self-esteem, and their fear is at the heart of the "battered women syndrome."

Can batterers change? In some cases women stay with their abusers because they believe that the men will stop. When the men express guilt after a beating, and plead with the women to stay, swearing that it will never happen again, the women believe them. Most often, however, the assaults continue. Is it possible for these men to stop physically abusing their partners? Experts disagree on this issue. Some believe that only if the men are arrested and receive counseling can they really change their behavior. A combination of "paying for the crime," and learning a harsh lesson by being placed in jail, plus confronting their behavior, is necessary for that behavior to stop.

Others argue that domestic violence will not stop unless society makes a concerted effort to reeducate men about behavior toward women. As long as boys and men feel that they can casually brag about beating up "their women," and that beating "their women" is a sign of control and macho status, some men will continue to believe that they have a right to act in that fashion.

We'll explore each of these myths more fully, as we look at this tragic problem further.

CHAPTER THREE

COURTSHIP AND ROMANCE: THE CYCLE OF ABUSE BEGINS

PATTY'S STORY

As I visited women's shelters and counseling centers while conducting research for this book, I began to see that many abused women described very similar experiences. Patty's story is a good example. She had met her husband years earlier when she was a young, pretty, and very shy young woman. An old photograph shows an appealing young woman with fragile features who looked innocent and as if she needed love and attention.

At a party, she met Jim, who came from the same small town. He was tall with handsome features and an intense look. She recalled their first meeting.

"He just walked over to me and began talking. I was flattered. I thought he was so handsome. I was twenty years old and I had dated very little. I came from a very strict background; my father ruled the house and didn't want me to go out with guys he didn't know or approve of."

Jim seemed different. He was older. He was very nice and showed a lot of care and concern.

"He drove me home and walked me to my door. My

father would approve of him. I knew that. He called me the next day and asked if he could take me to the movies and to dinner."

Then he sent her flowers. "No one ever sent me flowers. In fact, I hardly knew many guys who wanted to take you to the movies or had the money to take you to dinner. They all seemed to just want to sleep with you. Since I wasn't very interested, or was afraid, I wasn't very popular."

Jim seemed like a dream come true for Patty. Her father liked him, and that was very important. She wanted her father's approval. Her mother, on the other hand, just didn't trust him, but could not really put her finger on why. He did everything that any young girl in a small town with few options could have asked for.

They dated for almost a year. Jim was very romantic, very attentive, and Patty spent more and more time with him. He picked her up in the morning, and took her to the grocery store where she worked as a cashier, training to become an assistant manager. Often he came to pick her up after work. Things seemed heavenly for the first few months. No one had ever loved her this way. No one had ever paid her this much attention or showered her with flowers. When he asked to marry her, it was the best day of her life. She could not wait.

Her parents had very little money, so Jim said they would forget about a big wedding, and just go to the church and get married without making a fuss. Patty was relieved that her parents would not have to pay for a large wedding. She felt this was further proof Jim cared about her and wanted to make life easy for her and her parents. Jim's own mother was a widow and was happy to go along with their plans, but Patty's parents were unhappy about not being consulted, or asked how they felt about the wedding and if they wished to spend the money. Jim had decided for them.

She recalled her mother saying,"Honey, you get married only once. Why not wait a year, and save up the money, and then have your friends and your family with you. It's a big occasion in your life."

But Patty was very eager to get married and be with Jim. As she looked back she said she had wanted a big wedding but she had been afraid to say anything to Jim. She was afraid to offend him and worried that he might change his mind and not marry her.

Until their wedding, they had had few major arguments. Patty just went along with all his wishes and desires. "One day I had to work late and Jim came to pick me up. My store manager went out when he started honking the car horn and told Jim I had to work late. Jim waited for me for two hours until I got off work. He was furious."

Jim blew up and accused her of hanging out with the manager. He demanded that she ask permission from him first, if she ever needed to work late again. At twenty years of age, Patty was afraid to talk to him about it, but didn't really understand why he was so angry. She figured that it was just that he wanted to be with her.

The next major blowup came just before their wedding night. She had invited some of her friends to the wedding without first discussing it with him. Five of his male friends were invited so she really didn't find it wrong to invite her two best friends and her sister's boyfriend. Jim was furious.

"'What's wrong with Kathy and Sue?' I asked him. 'They are my best friends.'" He exploded, "I make those decisions around here and don't forget it, or you'll regret it." That was the first time that he threatened her. But Patty thought that he was nervous about the wedding. Then he threw her on the bed and made love to her. Just before he fell asleep, he whispered that he was sorry, and added, "But don't do that again." Patty recalled that it had been a nice wedding — plain, simple, and her mother had cried.

The first time that he hit her was a few months after they were married. She had gone out with her friends and called home to say she would be late. He was home, drinking beer. She walked in the door, smiling, and was about to kiss him. He smashed her head against the wall, punched her, pulled her hair, and shoved her into the kitchen. "So, where the hell is my dinner. You better fix me something good and fast."

Patty's mouth was bleeding and she ran into the bathroom to try to clean it up when he came at her again. As she fixed dinner, she began to sob. He said, "You better stop that, now. Stop all that silly carrying-on and get to that dinner. I mean it."

"He starting cursing at me as he ate his supper. I tried to explain. I said I was sorry. I had thought he was going to the bar to watch the ball game with the guys; otherwise I would have come home earlier. For several days it was tense around the house, but after a while he seemed to be ok. A few weeks later he bought me a nightgown that we had seen together, that he liked. 'Hey, you'll look gorgeous and sexy in this.' I loved it and I thanked him, again and again. In those days we made love a lot and I promised to wear it every time we made love."

Things seemed fine for a while. Patty stopped staying out with her friends. He didn't like it if she spent too much time with her girl friends. The next major incident occurred while she was pregnant with their first child.

"I was on the phone talking to one of my friends. Since I didn't go out with my girl friends very much, I wanted to at least talk with them. My best friend, Sue, was in a crisis with her boyfriend, so she called. She usually called when she knew Jim wasn't home, but this time she was very upset and called when he was there.

I didn't hear Jim calling me from the living room, since I was lying down upstairs in the bedroom. He came into the room and yanked the phone out of my hand, and yelled, 'Didn't you hear me talking to you, you damn bitch. You're not going to lie here and talk to your damn boyfriend in my house.' I was shocked. 'I'm talking to Sue, and you know I don't have a boyfriend. I am pregnant with our baby. What's wrong with you?' Again he smacked me and I cried. I slept on the living room couch that night but he came downstairs and told me to get into the bed or he'd really give me what I deserve."

"After that incident things changed for me. I felt differently. But I still loved him very much. I made excuses for his behavior and since it had happened only a few times, I figured that once the baby was born, he'd be happy and we'd be happy together." Jim had said that he wanted the baby and Patty was still anxious to please him.

According to Patty, Jim seemed very uncommunicative, moody, and withdrawn the first few months after the baby was born. Her mother came to help with the baby but Jim objected to that. He insisted that he didn't want her mother around, and since she was no longer working, she could take care of the child herself.

"I had a tough time telling my mother not to come to help me with the baby when I so desperately wanted her help and company. It was the only way that I could get some sleep or go to the store without dressing the baby and dragging her along."

One day, without telling him, her mother came and Patty took the opportunity to go out and buy food and take care of some chores. Jim had just called a little earlier to check on things, and she didn't expect him to call again so soon. So, she thought he'd never find out that her mother was there. Looking back, she says she should have told her mother not to answer the phone. But Jim did call, and found her mother there. That night he came home very late, and had been drinking. As soon as he walked in, he started to hit her with his fist, called her names, and threatened to really hurt her if she continued to disobey his orders. She barely knew what had happened.

Again, she blamed herself for what had occurred and swore to herself that she wouldn't do anything to upset him again. She was not badly bruised, and she told herself his anger had come from his dislike for her mother, who had not trusted him from the beginning and acted very distant from him.

In the first few years of their marriage the incidents had been rare, perhaps every few months, but as the years went by his tantrums became more frequent and unpredictable. Now the physical abuse became more severe. After each attack he apologized and tried to make up to her. One day he even helped with the dishes without being asked.

Patty's days were spent with her young daughter, her mother came rarely, and most of her friends knew not to bother her. Jim never brought home his friends, he seemed to spend more and more time with the guys, and she felt isolated and lonely. She suggested to him that they could really use some more money and she wanted to go back to work — at least part-time. He simply hit the roof, Patty recalled.

"Why, this ain't good enough for you? What kind of mother are you? You want to leave a three year old baby?" He went on screaming, telling her that she was a poor mother and not much of a wife. She felt totally devastated. She had no friends, not much contact with her family, her husband was rarely home, and she wanted to get out of the house. The next time she brought up the subject, he threw some dishes at her. Their child woke up screaming, frightened and confused. Patty wanted to leave that night and go to her parents' house, but was afraid. The phone rang. It was his mother.

Patty recalls, "Thank God she called. That night I came very close to just grabbing the child and leaving, but I knew that he would follow me and it would just be worse."

One evening, after several months of peace, he was home when without any provocation, he blew up, told her that she was a stupid, fat, ugly bitch that no one wanted, and that she should be happy to have him care for her and her baby. That night, he didn't hit her, but she remembered his words and she felt that she was looking fat and unkempt. She hardly ever left the house except to take the child to a nursery, to go shopping, or take care of household chores.

"Honey, you said I was getting fat." Patty remembers saying. "I'd like to go to a weight loss program so I'll look the way you'd like me to look." Patty was startled when he flew across the room and with his full strength started beating her, and screaming, "Why, you've a new boyfriend? You're seeing a guy behind my back?"

This night she was beaten severely, while the child, not yet asleep, was afraid to come out of her room. Patty was so bruised that she could not take her daughter to school. Jim took her to school instead and Patty had to ask her mother to pick her up because he was working. Her mother came in to talk with Patty, to console her, and to try to help her to stop the beatings. Her mother was appalled, but she didn't suggest that Patty leave him.

After five years of this cycle of beatings and apologies, Patty decided that she had to get a hold of her life. She no longer tried to please him at all costs, because she felt that there was no way she could prevent the beatings. She could only try to make them less frequent.

After his job was reduced and he earned less money, she did go back to work — but only part-time. He still objected but she presented it as a way to take some pressure off him. He hated her working and warned that she had better take care of everything else or he would not permit her to work. While she says she never fought back, her part-time job gave her a little freedom and some time away from home, with some other people. At first she went straight home after work and tried to have dinner ready before he returned. He still hated the idea that she was not home when he called and he could not call her at work. Years passed, with occasional beatings.

She ended up in the emergency room for the first time seven years after their marriage. There had been countless beatings that had caused black eyes, bruises and cuts, and some bleeding. But this time he shoved her against the wall, causing a lamp to fall on her and cut her head. After the doctor took care of her cuts, including one that required several stitches, the hospital personnel asked what had happened. Jim was standing next to her. She lied and said that the lamp had fallen on her accidentally. But the doctor, who had been trained to be alert for evidence of domestic abuse, examined her and found that there were just too many bruises to have been caused by a falling lamp. The social worker, who had gone to school with Patty, called her at home the next day and Patty told her the whole story. The social worker gave her the phone number of a hot line for battered women. Patty, like over 90 percent of abused women, had never dared call the police.

Again Jim promised, and convinced her, that it would never happen again. And again, she convinced herself that she believed him. But now, she had a permanent scar on her head and felt even more bound to him, for surely no one else would want her now.

Some months later, at the start of another attack, she called the battered women's hot line and, as suggested, moved to her parents' home. But after just a few days, she returned home. On the average, it takes seven tries before a battered woman finally manages to leave her home. Patty had not reached that point, yet.

Patty's story is typical. She had loved her husband when they first married and they had many good times together. She felt loved and needed by him and believed that no one else would want her or love her the way he did. At first he was a good father, and a fairly good breadwinner. Later, he changed. Her expectations were very low, corresponding to her low sense of self esteem — a common characteristic of abused women. She gradually became more isolated and his jealousies that had, at first, seemed to be signs of love became irrational and abusive.

Eventually Patty had gone to a safe house for battered women for counseling, and had told her story to a counselor in the program. However, Patty had dropped out of the program, and no one in the battered women's center knows what has become of her.

CHAPTER FOUR

WHY DO WOMEN STAY?

ROSE'S STORY

The question people ask most often is why do women stay in a home or relationship where they are abused. One friend's comments are typical: "I am sorry, but I really have no sympathy for a woman who stays with a man after repeated beatings and abuse. We're not living in some part of the world where women's fathers sell them off to their husbands, and where they would have no way to survive on their own."

In the United States and Canada and many other countries, women have full opportunities to go to school and achieve independence. So, it is truly difficult to accept the fact that a large number of women are indeed being battered, and that they continue to stay with their batterer — even to the point that many end up dead.

Women remain with abusers because of psychological, economic, and social reasons. Most importantly, they are afraid of the abuser. They are afraid for their lives. This fear rules their actions.

As my unsympathetic friend had put it, "If he hit me once, I'd be gone. I'd leave him in a minute." However, these women have several psychological characteristics that make it very difficult for them to conceive of leaving. Like Patty, they often have low self-esteem. Sometimes through years of abuse, the husbands or partners have terrorized them into believing that the women cannot get along without them, and the women are afraid of what would happen to them if they left. Many of the women accept the blame for their husbands' actions, and they believe that no one can really help them. These women cannot imagine any alternative.

Rose, is one example. I met her at a battered women's shelter. She had been married to Ramon for twelve years. Their first years together were rather typical for a man and a woman from Hispanic backgrounds, who married young and had several children early in their marriage. She had three young children and worked part-time. Her husband was an auto mechanic who worked fairly steadily and had a strong belief in the traditional, male-dominated family.

Very early in the marriage, Ramon began to display a violent temper. Little things annoyed him. When the first child was an infant, it woke up a lot at night. The baby's crying set him off quickly.

Rose, who had been brought up to believe that pleasing her husband was her first responsibility, didn't know what she was doing wrong. She talked with her mother, who was used to "minor" abuse over the years from her husband, Rose's stepfather. Her mother suggested that she make sure that the baby did not wake up Ramon at night. Rose should either put the baby in the other room at night or sleep in the same room as the baby, ready to quiet it quickly. Rose tried that. One night Ramon woke up, found that she was not in their bed, and came to where she was sleeping and, without any discussion, hit her hard. She couldn't understand why he had hit her. After all, she had been trying to keep him happy by making sure that he was not awakened by the baby's crying.

Before she could say anything, Ramon began to yell. "You don't care about me anymore. All you want to do is hold that baby of yours. Don't you know what you're supposed to do as my wife?" She tried to say that she had wanted only to keep him from being bothered, but he shut her up.

When she discussed the incident with her mother, her mother shrugged her shoulders, and said that this is what women have to accept. She told Rose to try to figure out how to keep Ramon happy and make him feel he was getting her attention, and still take care of the baby.

As is common in many abusive relationships, Ramon was jealous and wanted Rose's attention all the time. Abusers — living with their own very low level of self-esteem — often need reassurance from their "woman" that they are the only thing that is important, and that all their desires will be met by the woman. With these dynamics operating, the birth of a child often triggers the onset of battering. A baby, naturally, needs much of the mother's attention and time, which means there is less available for the man.

Rose's life with Ramon didn't get better. For the first few years, she tried very hard to keep peace at home. She learned what might provoke him to beat her and tried to use her wits to forestall an attack. Like most women in abusive relationships, Rose at first believed she could prevent explosive incidents.

Many women claim they learn to recognize the pattern to the incidents of abuse. First, the men start picking on little things. It could be the baby's crying, or it could be that the wife forgot to put a beer in the refrigerator before he came home, or that she bought the wrong beer, even though it was on sale and the previous week he had exploded because she had bought the more expensive brand.

This period may be called the "tension building

phase," and it can last for quite a while. But the women already are anticipating the second phase in this cycle: the eruption of anger and a fight. After the physical abuse, the men tend to go through the third phase, the guilty or tender phase, when they try to convince the women that it will never happen again.

Many women cover up their bruises, or deny that they received a black eye, or were seriously hurt to protect their partners. Some excuse the hitting, saying it was really their fault, and they should have done, or not done, whatever prompted the explosion. They also enjoy the tenderness offered during the "make up" cycle. Sometimes during this period of loving, the memory of hurt fades away.

Rose says that she really didn't experience much of the tender or guilty period. Ramon would say that he was sorry, but he never accepted responsibility for having done something wrong. He believed that he had the right to hit her and that she would never stop him from hitting her.

Rose's second baby was born a year after her first one. The two children kept her busy and they both cried during the night, something Rose tried to conceal from her husband. She sat up with them at night, trying to keep them from crying and waking him, knowing that if he should wake up and not find her by his side, he would start yelling and have a tantrum. But she also knew that he sometimes stayed out late drinking, and then would usually fall asleep as soon as he got home and not wake up if the babies cried. She almost welcomed the times when he would come home late and go to sleep. The alcohol would make him more irritable but it also made him go right to sleep.

Throughout this time Rose never considered leaving him. The abuse did not occur that often, although Ramon was often moody, demanding, and hard to please. He wanted everything his way. And Rose could not predict what would set him off or why he would get angry, because they could never talk about this problem.

About two years later, a third child was born, five years after she and Ramon had married. One hot summer evening, Rose was sitting on the stoop of her building with her three children. She was talking to someone she knew from the neighborhood, when Ramon came home from a bar. She thought that he was drunk. He pulled her hair, pushed her upstairs to their apartment and, with her three small children by her side, he beat her hard enough to cause bleeding. As she tried to call the police, something that she had never done before (only about 10 percent of abused women ever resort to calling the police), he yanked the phone from the wall and threw it at her. The phone missed her, but she was thrown against the wall. The neighbors heard the fighting and notified the police.

Two white police officers arrived and looked at her and the children as if they had bigger crimes to fight. They asked if there was any problem. She replied, "No, it was just an accident."

"An accident?" the officer repeated, as Rose recalls this incident now. While the officer did not seem to believe that it was a question of an accident, he also did nothing except warn them that there better not be any more "noise" from their apartment.

"Why did you say that it was an accident" I asked Rose. "You must be kidding" she replied. "If I had said he was beating me, I was afraid that he'd kill me as soon as they left."

She was echoing what most abused women have said: unless the police officers take the man away, or move the woman into a shelter out of reach of the man, the police are leaving the woman in serious danger. Now the abuser feels that she has humiliated him and embarrassed him in his own home.

In Rose's case, although she had not called the

police, once they left, her husband turned on her, hitting her even harder than before.

"See what you have done? You are causing me trouble in my own house, you slut." She hit him back weakly, but she realized that this made him even angrier.

The next incident landed her in the emergency room of a New York City municipal hospital. After treatment, she was released and sent home. But she was also given the name of a women's shelter. She could not manage to file charges against him. She could not bear to have her husband put in jail after all the horror stories she had heard about life inside a jail. She also knew that her family would ostracize her for doing that to the father of her children.

So, she took the children, and left him while he was at work, and she moved in with her mother and her stepfather. "I knew that he would never hit me while I was at my mother's house. He never hit me anywhere but at home. When he got home he called me at my mother's. I told him that I was not coming home with the children unless he promised never to hit me again. I meant it.

"He came over and told my mother that he never meant to hurt me, that he loved me, and that I was fooling around with some guy in the neighborhood and humiliating him, so he had to 'teach me a lesson.'" Rose hadn't been doing anything with any man. She could barely work and take care of her three children. But abusive men often offer explanations that their woman is cheating on them as a justification of their behavior.

Rose's mother didn't believe Ramon, but she wanted her daughter to go back with him to give him another chance. Neither she nor Rose could see any other option. Rose could not support the three children by herself; there was no telling what Ramon might do if she tried to divorce him nor was it likely that he would send her any money for support. After a few weeks of staying with her mother, she made the painful decision to go back with him, hoping that his promises of "I'll never do it again," would be true.

Several years later, Ramon beat Rose and threatened her with a knife so that she feared for her life. She grabbed her children, told him she was leaving, and warned that she would call the police and have him put in jail if he came near her. That frightened him long enough for her to get the knife from his hand, and then she fled.

Ramon had told her that night that if she tried to divorce him, he would come and kill her and she fears that one day he might still do that. She has obtained a temporary court order of protection against him, which forbids him to come near her. She has charged him with assault and battery, however she doesn't think a court order will stop him from coming after her. She quit her job and is living in a shelter with her children and a dozen other women and children with painfully similar stories. Rose is looking for a place to stay after the short 90-day stay provided by the shelter is up. She has taken her children out of the school they have attended for years to keep him from finding them. She is trying to keep one step ahead of him.

For now, he is ordered by the courts to stay away from her, but she knows that soon the court will grant him visitation rights to see the children that he had never seemed to care about before. Her mother still hopes she will try to work things out and go home to Ramon. Her step father thinks that she should just go and have a tough talk with Ramon.

But Rose, after some twelve years of abuse, is determined not to go back. She wants her own life and a way to help her three children who have been traumatized by the family violence and by her fleeing from their father. She doesn't know where it will all end. She thinks of getting a gun, but fears that she might not have the chance to use it. She knows her husband wants revenge for her leaving.

Rose's story is still unfolding or, as her counselor in the shelter puts it, this tragedy is not yet over. If she finds a place and moves from the shelter, what are the chances that Ramon won't find her and begin the battering again? What protection can the court really give someone like Rose? She cannot keep where she lives a secret. If he gets visitation rights to the children, how can she continue to hide from him? If Ramon finds her, what is to stop him from beating up this woman who has left him and betrayed him?

So, why don't abused women just leave? As we can see in Rose's case, the relationship evolved and the violence escalated to a dangerous level. The reality of economic circumstances adds to the problem. As with most women in similar circumstances, Rose doesn't want to go on welfare. She has never been on welfare and she hates the social stigma attached to welfare. Yet, she cannot support her children and cannot go back to her mother's house with them. She thinks that she will find a place to move and that she will separate from her husband. She prays to just stay alive and take care of her children. But she herself cannot say if she will change her mind and just go back.

"Do you believe that he will come after you and hurt you?" I asked. "Oh, yes. I know that I won't ever be free from him, unless he's in jail or I kill him. It may not be that he'll come now, but, I know that he will find me. I just don't know how it will end. One of us just may have to die." So, that's why some women don't leave.

Charlotte Watson, the director of a well-known domestic violence program, states the problem very clearly. "Imagine that a stranger came into your house at night and attacked you, and you went to court and the judge said, 'We found the perpetrator who attacked you, and we have a very good case against him, so we can lock him up for his crime, but we need you to testify against him.' After thinking about it you'd say 'sure.' You would want to see him put away for what he did to you.

"But then imagine that the judge added, 'Well, there are just a few things that you need to know. For the rest of your life, you'll have to let him know where you are, you'll have to see him regularly and let him see your children, you will not be able to leave the state without letting him know where you are going.' Would you still want to testify against him? But, that's exactly what the woman has to do, and add to the situation the fact that the attacker is not a stranger, but the man she has loved."

According to Charlotte Watson and others who work with battered women, if a woman wants a divorce, often the abuser won't agree to one and she has to take him to court. If she brings up the abuse, the judge may decide that they both are not fit parents and she herself may lose custody of the child. If she gets custody, he can get visitation rights to see the children. He must be informed about where they live, and she cannot leave the state without getting his approval to take the children with her.

If she has a court order of protection against him, and he violates the court order to stay away from her, he might be put into jail. Then she will have to deal with her family, and the children. And if he is placed in jail, the term is usually brief, and while in jail, he can't even help support the children financially.

As we can see, it is a very difficult and complex situation. No one wants to go through the many problems that leaving home will cause for all involved. Some women have fought back and called the police, but most women have found that their attempts were feeble against an enraged male and it only aggravated the situation.

We will never find out what happened to other women who have left. Did they just run away, or did they manage to get a divorce without an incident that involved a medical emergency room or the police?

The only women we know about are those who have sought help, or who have been abused seriously enough to come to the attention of the authorities. Unfortunately, when some abusive relationships end, the men start up a new relationship, and often begin the same cycle with another woman.

HOW CAN WOMEN AVOID ABUSIVE RELATIONSHIPS?

Some of you may have lived in a household poisoned by an abusive parent. You may have watched helplessly as your mother was hit by her partner, perhaps your father. Too often, you, the innocent children, were also part of the abuse, when the man and, at times, the woman took out their anger and frustration on you.

This experience usually traumatizes children, making them dysfunctional, and causing them to fail in school. These children need help. Too often men who abuse their wives or partners also commit incest with their daughters and sometimes even with their sons. The family suffers under a rule of terror. The children grow up in circumstances of violence that can often continue through teenage years into adulthood.

A teenage girl will swear that this will never happen to her, and that she will never stay with a man who hits her. But sometimes, teenage relationships can develop in later years into abusive ones. Perhaps the warning indications cannot be clearly identified in teenage relationships because there is no violence. Yet inequality in the relationship between the boy and girl may already exist, and an abusive relationship may start to develop before one realizes what's happening.

Charlotte Watson is director of My Sister's Place, a shelter for abused women with an advocacy program for victims of domestic violence. My Sister's Place, like many other shelters and agencies, seeks to educate youngsters of all ages by conducting seminars in the schools on the warning signs of an abusive relationship. These programs hope to reach some of the boys and girls before violence begins and becomes their way of life.

Charlotte Watson presents the following scenario to girls in a high school seminar: A boy whom you have been really wanting to go out with, calls and asks you for a date. You get off the phone, excited and happy because you are going out with this popular guy. He could date any girl, but he asked you. So you must be special. He tells you that he'll come and pick you up on Friday at 8 P.M. and that he'll take you to see *Cliffhanger*, and then for a pizza. You just can't wait. You are excited, and as soon as he gets off the phone, you call your friends and tell them all about it. The great news! Date with Mr. Right.

So far this sounds like a perfect teenage date — except you were afraid to say that 8 P.M. will be a problem for your mother because you are supposed to be home by 11:30 P.M. on Friday nights. If you went to an earlier show, it would have been a lot better for you. You are excited about the date, although you saw that movie last week. He didn't ask you if any of this was OK with you, but in the rush of excitement, you were just happy to say yes.

Clearly, it is a big leap from a great guy who asks you to the movies to a man who abuses a wife or partner. But keep in mind that abusive relationships do not begin as abusive. In fact, many of these guys are very charming and loving and give the women a great deal of attention.

Counselors warn, however, that if a guy takes you out and never asks where you want to go, what you want to do, when you need to be home and, finally, whether you want to have sex, an abusive relationship could be developing. This is controlling behavior and very often, the man's need to dominate "his woman" leads to the cycle of abuse.

You might think, "In that case, I may never have a date in high school with a popular guy. If I don't go along with what he wants, he'll just ask another girl out." That may be true, but, "going along" with all his wishes can lead to a relationship where your desires are ignored, and you are treated without respect.

To avoid a pattern of abuse from begining, it is important to help guys understand that while you want to date them and spend time with them, they also have to consider your ideas and feelings, and do some of the things that you want to do.

SOME WARNING SIGNALS

"But, how can I tell from dating a guy whether or not he is going to end up being a violent man?" This is the question often asked in the group sessions that many of the domestic-violence prevention programs conduct in schools for teenagers. The counselor leading one group responded, "You cannot tell for sure, but you need to be aware of the signs."

Unfortunately, there is no exact blueprint to follow to avoid ending up with an abusive man. While no one can predict with certainty who will be an abuser before he has been violent, some patterns of behavior can serve as warnings.

These signs indicate patterns often seen in the behavior of abusers. Watch out for:
- an extraordinary need for control,
- extreme jealousy,
- wild mood swings,
- an overabundance of charm and loving behavior,
- manipulation of the woman,

- withdrawal of the love when their partner does not obey the man's wishes,
- threats and verbal abuse.

In addition, excessive drinking or drug abuse are contributing factors, though many experts do not see them as a cause of violence, but rather as an exacerbating influence.

Men who exhibit extreme jealousy and possessiveness may be very domineering. The jealousy may disguise a terrible need for control, and not be just a show of love. During the teenage years, jealousy is a normal part of the dating game, so it can be very difficult to distinguish between expressions of love and a need for exclusive attention. A person who changes suddenly without any warning — who is charming one moment and angry the next — may be a potential abuser.

Another important warning sign is the repeated need to undermine their girlfriends' accomplishments by constantly making fun of them or putting them down. Many men abuse their lovers or partners by minimizing their achievements, making hurtful comments, and embarrassing them. They may punish by withdrawing their love, or money, or attention.

THE EARLY STAGES OF AN ABUSIVE RELATIONSHIP

Let's examine how a typical relationship develops gradually into one of abuse and domination. Imagine you really care about a guy you have been seeing, and he decides to move to another state to get a job. You tell him that while you'll see him whenever he can come to town, or you'll call him and write to him, you do not want to leave your home and go where he is going. He answers, "All right, we'll just get married and then you will have to go where I say we go."

You don't want to lose him and you may even have

been hoping to marry him, so you find yourself saying yes. No one can say that this man will end up being abusive, but already some of the need for power and control, so basic to these battering relationships, is apparent.

By putting the woman into isolating circumstances, he sets up a situation in which he has power over her. Your boy friend wants to move to another state where he knows some people, and can get a job. But you don't know anyone there and will not find a job easily.

Now, you're totally dependent on him for emotional needs and economic needs and, since you are isolated from family, friends, and other contacts, you are dependent on him socially as well.

SEXIST VIOLENCE IN THE HIGH SCHOOLS

According to studies of battering relationships, more than one in eight teenagers experience physical violence in their dating relationships. Young men may think it is macho to "teach their girlfriend a lesson," or show who is in charge. These are warning signs. Some of the these people will become batterers of women.

A study conducted in 1993 by Louis Harris and Associates for the American Association of University Women's Education Foundation found that harassment of female students has become the norm in high school. As one high school student put it, it's "just part of school life."

One of the alarming findings of the study was that according to the boys interviewed, a lot of guys see sexual harassment and abuse as bonding rituals. A teenage boy echoing the views of others said, "If you see people slapping their girl, they probably get respect from the other boys." They believe that if a boy is caught treating a girl well, he will lose the approval of his friends. Girls seem to accept the notion that their boyfriend will not even acknowledge them in public. In turn, the girls felt that often they would not trust a boy enough to go out with him anyway.

According to this study of over 1,600 students in 79 schools across the country, rituals of abuse have replaced youthful courtship. Apparently, young people do not want a "relationship." The boys believe that they gain popularity by fondling and abusing girls and by calling them names like "bitches." The girls seem to have accepted that romantic relationships are rare and not worth the trouble.

The New York Times, citing this study, noted, "Fear, and the desire of boys to demonstrate their manhood by abusing or showing disrespect to girls, was repeated time and again in more than 50 interviews with teenagers. . . . Teenagers said that either they don't date or don't admit to it. According to one of the nineteen-year-old girls from the Bronx, 'Nobody loves nobody anymore. And there's no respect, no trust.' Another seventeen-year-old teenager referring to verbal and physical abuse noted that you see a lot of sunglasses and black eyes."

The view of one fourteen-year-old girl from New Jersey revealed great sadness. "It makes me think if I get in a relationship he'll just call me a bitch." She is not hopeful. In her mind, boys just want as many girls as possible. The language that these teenagers use reveals that they do not see each other as people. If boys refer to girls as "bitches" and worse, and girls call boys "dogs," and sex a "function," then human life seems to have little or no value at all. The notion of loving someone seems to be rarely considered.

THE FUTURE

Those who work with victims of domestic violence see a direct and very strong connection between these attitudes and domestic violence. They question whether these teenagers will accept the idea of loving anyone and having a relationship based on caring and respect. The counselors insist that society must work to change these attitudes and they cite the campaign against cigarette smoking as a model of how society can successfully change attitudes.

Charlotte Watson of My Sister's Place, along with other counselors of women abused by domestic violence, believes the same type of public awareness needs to be created in order to reduce the imbalance of power between men and women and therefore reduce the amount of domestic violence. We must reinforce the message to all that society will not accept men's violence against women, and will punish those that commit the abuse.

An ugly situation that occurred in the public pools of New York City in the summer of 1993 illustrates the behavior and attitudes of teenage boys that must be changed. The pool was filled with hundreds of people. A fourteen-year-old girl was swimming, when a gang of boys tore off her bathing suit and began to fondle her. She screamed but her cries could not be heard above the noise of people yelling and playing in the pool. What was astonishing was that many teenage girls commented that this activity called the "whirlpool" was common. Many of the teenage boys regularly harassed young girls.

ENDING THE RELATIONSHIP
BEFORE IT BEGINS

Just think about how difficult it is to break up with someone you really love, and who says he loves you in return. You want to spend the rest of your life with him, and he says he feels that way about you. At times he is abusive, yet at other times he is loving. He cares so much that he doesn't ever want you out of his sight and he doesn't want another man to touch you. He wants you to do as he says because he is the MAN.

Although this relationship is hard to give up, you are not yet dependent on him for your survival. You don't have children with him, and you have not yet built a home with him. Just imagine this same situation two, three, or five years from now, when he controls your movements, your life, your ability to work and to purchase food, to see a friend or your family. Now, he has also begun to verbally abuse you and scream at you when he is unhappy with something. On occasion, if you don't follow his commands at home, he resorts to violence.

That seems to be the pattern seen in many of the relationships. They do not begin with abuse, but over time as the women become more psychologically and economically dependent on their partner, the classic pattern of domestic violence emerges.

So, how do you avoid abusive relationships? Protect yourself by paying attention to early warning signals. Do not diminish the significance of your own feelings, needs, and misgivings. Do not accept easy excuses for violent behavior, such as "boys will be boys." Do not accept unfair and unwarranted criticism, and attacks on your self-worth.

If the early danger signs are present, end a relationship even if you love someone.

CHAPTER SIX

LEGAL PROTECTIONS

Domestic violence is is not a new problem in the world. In the past, men were legally permitted to beat their wives. According to Blackstone's 1768 codification of English laws, a husband was allowed to beat his wife with a stick, or switch, as long as it was no thicker than his thumb. In 1824 in the United States, a Mississippi law provided that a husband could hit his wife, but on a restricted basis: "moderate chastisement in cases of emergency." This law stood until 1894. In 1874, the Supreme Court of North Carolina banned the "finger switch rule," as it was known, and stated that "the husband has no right to chastise his wife under any circumstances."

By the beginning of the twentieth century in England, a wife who had been habitually beaten by her husband to the point that her life was endangered was allowed by law to separate from him, although she was not allowed to divorce him. At the same time, a law was passed prohibiting a husband from selling his wife or daughter into prostitution.

In France, wife beating was a man's right until 1924. Iran and Scotland did not declare wife beating illegal until the 1970s. In Brazil wives were considered a man's property until 1975, when renting, selling, or gambling away wives was prohibited. With these laws and attitudes regarding women as our legacy, it is not surprising that some men believe that they are entitled to treat women as they please.

Not until the late 1970s did most states in the United States have any laws providing relief for victims of domestic violence. Until that time domestic violence was treated as a private matte

In the past the police were reluctant to arrest abusers and dreaded being called to interfere in domestic violence situations. Since the laws were vague or non–existent, often all the police could do was issue a warning to the couple. Once the police left, the woman was often further abused, or punished for calling the police.

Since the late 1970s, a great deal of progress has been made in providing legal remedies for domestic abuse. Today, all states and the District of Columbia have statutes authorizing civil orders of protection for victims of domestic violence. In the past, these protection orders were very limited in scope and rarely enforced. The national trend is now to expand coverage given by these protection orders. For example, in 1983 only 17 states provided protection against abuse for an unmarried partner living with a person as a spouse. In 1988, that protection had been made available in 39 states. This is very important in an era of high divorce rates when a large number of people who live together as partners are not legally married. All these people need protection against abuse also.

Another example of expanded protection is a Minnesota statute that provides relief from domestic violence for spouses, former spouses, parents, children, persons related by blood, persons who have a child in common, and persons who are presently residing together or who have resided together in the past. If a man abuses a woman whom he no longer lives with, or has never married, or who has filed for a divorce or has left home, the court can still offer protection to the woman.

Many new laws and procedures relating to abuse have been passed in recent years. The laws are complex and vary from state to state, as does the definition of domestic violence. The state of Washington, for example, defines domestic violence in the broadest sense; assault, reckless endangerment, coercion, burglary, malicious mischief and imprisonment. Twenty-nine states also include sexual assault of an adult, involuntary sexual relations, force, and threat of force within the definition of abuse.

In addition, most states no longer require a victim to petition for protection within a specific time limit. In Oregon, the courts will consider petitions from people claiming to have been abused within the preceding 180 days. This could be crucial for a woman who is too intimidated to file for protection while she is living in her abuser's house. She can make arrangements to move and then file for a protection order as soon as she has left, so that if he finds her, he will not feel free to continue to abuse her. Waiting to seek protection can work against the victim, however. The longer a victim waits, the more difficult it is to prove that she has been abused.

Although new and much improved laws do help abuse victims, the laws are often hard to enforce. To use legal remedies, the victims must first get from the court an emergency or temporary order for protection. To do this, the victim needs to demonstrate to the court that she is in immediate danger or that irreparable injury is likely to occur. As soon as this order is served, the abuser can be temporarily removed from the house and told that if he violates the court order, he can be sentenced to serve time in jail.

In many cases, however, the woman may need to enter a hospital for treatment. The police may have to find the abuser before serving him with the protection order. Temporary orders for protection do not deal with the major issues of child visitation or property ownership. Their purpose is just immediate safety for the victim.

Unfortunately, a court order is not a guarantee of protection, as I discovered in my interviews. I can still hear the mocking voices of the women who described their experiences. One said, "Oh please, I had an order of protection, and then he came back and beat me up. I ended up in the hospital emergency room, and then the social worker referred me to this shelter."

Another woman spoke. "I had an order of protection. I called the police, and they removed him. The next day he came to my work place. He waited for me after work, shoved me into his car, and raped me in the back seat. He told me that if I didn't drop the order for protection and let him back in, I wouldn't find my children at home the next day, that he'd pick them up and I'd never see them again. I believed him." It took another two years before this woman called the police again and fled to a shelter with her children. She is now debating whether or not to leave the area and move to another state.

Monitoring and enforcement of court orders remains difficult. With court calendars overcrowded and prison systems filled to the limits, the overburdened justice system doesn't treat domestic violence as a high priority. Furthermore, police often have difficulty tracking down abusers. But the abusers know the daily patterns of their wives or partners, and they know who their friends and family members are. If they want to, they will find the women sooner or later. When the men do, the abuse – the punishment– is often very serious and sometimes fatal. Remember, one third of female homicide victims have been killed by their husbands or boyfriends. Women are nine times more likely than men to be the victim of a violent act inside their home, rather than on the streets.[1] And according to the March of Dimes, more women lose their babies due to physical abuse than for any medical reason.

Why don't more women initiate civil or criminal proceedings against their abusers? First, many women who are abused have no idea that in most states they can get an emergency order for protection. Many women fear that an order of protection might anger the abuser and make the situation worse. They are afraid of the possible retaliation. Other women feel they cannot request a court order because the matter is private; they are embarrassed and do not want the state involved.

Many battered women do not trust that their abuser will abide by the court order, or that the police will enforce it. In small communities, women feel that the police side with the men. Often, the men and the police know each other and are sports buddies, or drinking partners and friends. The women feel that the police are indifferent or hostile and don't believe that they are abused. But the fact remains that laws exist, in nearly all states, that require that the men be removed if they are abusing a partner and are to serve time in jail if they do not abide by a court order.

It is also very difficult for a woman fleeing a violent man to find a safe place to hid. The Family Violence Act of 1988 provides funds to help strengthen victims' resources, including police assistance in domestic violence situations, and to finance some much needed research into the problem. However, it did not provide any additional funds for shelters, although these are crucial for women seeking to escape violence. In 1980, there was practically no place where a woman could find emergency refuge. Today, there are over 1,500 women's shelters. Nevertheless, this is a very small number for the several million women who are victims of abuse each year.[2]

When women do finally decide to leave, they need

assistance to make their departure a final one. The women need help with filing legal papers to apply for permanent protection. They may need money for court fees. An attorney is necessary to seek a permanent protection order beyond the 30 or 90 days of a temporary order. If children are involved, the court must ensure orderly visits, without violence or abuse. Women may need a place to hide for a period of time, unless they can feel safe in a friend or relative's house. These women need emotional support from counselors, and practical help with starting a new life and, often, public assistance for at least a period of time.[3]

Emotional strength and stability are needed through all the steps of ending an abusive relationship. The police may not take women seriously because the police claim that women often start the process and then don't carry it through to the end. Often after the police arrive, the women drop the charges against the abusers. The police feel their time is wasted in responding to calls to intervene in domestic violence affairs that end up with women making up with their abusers. Some police who have received special training have a better understanding of what happens in domestic abuse, and why the women often cannot go through with filing charges and taking the men to court. More police are becoming aware of the fear the women live in.

If a woman can call the police, or contact an abuse hot line and go to a shelter, she eventually may be able to put the years of abuse behind her. In some cases, the court order and the threat of a jail sentence do frighten a man enough. He lets the woman leave and no longer bothers her once she has moved. Often, the man finds a new girlfriend and the original wife or partner is no longer the object of his obsession.

Some of the women who leave an abusive relationship get involved with other men. Unfortunately, many of these women again become involved with men who abuse them. Other women are able to develop healthier relationships. And still others say that they will never again get involved in a relationship with a man. They just want peace and to be able to live without fear.

I asked the women I saw in shelters what they wanted me to include in a book about domestic violence. They all responded with one plea. "Please be sure to say that the women did not stay because they wanted or asked or liked to be abused. They stayed because they were afraid to leave, or did not know how to go about leaving."

Many of the abused women are immigrants or do not speak English well. They are unaware that laws in this country could help them. In their countries laws against domestic violence and court protection against abuse are unknown. And many of the women interviewed were emotionally devastated and did not think that they had the strength or independence to permanently leave the men. They lived in despair and often considered suicide.

We must help provide the American public with information that will help change the lives of abused women. Abuse of women at home is a public matter and it affects all of us. No one should suffer in silence, alone, at home.

What's Love Got to Do With It, the film version of Tina Turner's autobiography, presents a graphic look at a woman — a superstar in this case — who was a victim of her husband's abuse. After years of abuse, Tina has managed to leave her husband. Now, starting her comeback, she is ready to perform in Madison Square Garden as a solo act, without her husband and costar. Just moments before she is due to go onstage, her estranged husband comes into her dressing room and threatens her with a gun. Calmly she looks at him. Strong and determined she says, "What are you going to do, shoot me?" After a tense moment when we in the audience wonder if indeed he will shoot, she turns and goes onstage. It is this kind of strength and courage that a woman would need to confront an abuser. Tina Turner survived the abuse, the threats, and the violence. But many, or in fact most, women are not able to dare the men to shoot them. And unfortunately, many of the men would have pulled the gun's trigger.

CHAPTER SEVEN

WHO ARE THE BATTERERS?

Angela Browne writes in *When Battered Women Kill*, "Violent men do search desperately for their partners once the woman leaves. Often, they spend their days and nights calling her family and mutual acquaintances; phoning her place of employment or showing up there; driving around the streets looking for her; haunting school grounds, playgrounds, and grocery stores; if they believe the woman has left town, they frequently attempt to follow her, traveling to all locations where they think she might be found. She is theirs. She cannot leave. They may nearly kill their mates, but they do not want to lose them."[1]

A woman may have been separated from the man for years, yet the man continues to harass her, threaten her, and follow her.

"Can you tell me about the men?" I asked a group of women in a shelter in a suburban community in Westchester, outside of New York City. "Who are they? What were they like? What made you stay with them?"

Three of the women began by talking about the extreme jealousy exhibited by the men who abused them.

"When you are young, you think that it's cute when a guy is jealous. It means he cares about you, and doesn't want you go anywhere, or see anyone. But let me

50

tell you, when you live with him, that stuff gets pretty bad," said Judy, a twenty-nine-year-old African-American woman, who had been severely beaten by a man she had left four years earlier. She'd been with him from the time she was fifteen years old, and called him her first best friend. Judy had had a son with him, and the son was with her now in the shelter.

Inez, a woman in her thirties, with two beautiful children, said her husband had almost choked her to death during the last episode of violence.

"I could not even go to the store. If I was late, he'd be looking out the window. If I looked in a store window, I must be looking at a guy. He called from work every hour. I stopped seeing my mother because he convinced me that my family was not supportive of me. Actually, they were not supportive of my relationship with him, but I was too stupid to realize what was happening."

Then she showed me what looked like a large diamond ring. "I got this last year after one of those fits of anger when he nearly choked me."

Inez, the most visibly angry of the women, told how she had obtained a restraining order against her husband, and then had him arrested. He was jailed for three weeks, which gave her the necessary time to gather her belongings and leave. When he was released from jail, he didn't know where to find her. She and her children had moved to the shelter.

"What you have to understand about these men is that they are like other men," added another woman, Michelle. "It's just that they are more extreme about everything. They have hot tempers, they are afraid to show affection so they convince you that they hit you because they care. They want everything the way they want it. It's OK for them to have another woman, to stay out at night. But you are theirs, so you have to be there at their every beck and call—their whipping girl.

They want to love you, and have sex when the last thing you want to do is hug them, kiss them, or make love to them. Then comes the next problem. They can feel that you don't want them to touch you, that you hate them, at least at that particular moment."

Still another woman, Lydia, spoke up. "Oh, yes. You've just been hit, and you're sore. Now he's sorry and he wants to be assured that you still want him sexually. So now you have to make love to him. And if you don't, then he is convinced that you're seeing another man, because you don't want him anymore. It's a vicious cycle."

"Whatever you write about, don't forget the jealousy thing." Judy said. Several of the other women agreed, telling me to emphasize the extreme nature of the men's possessiveness and jealousy.

"The problem with jealousy is that it is so normal, and everyone is jealous when they love someone," Judy continued. "At first, the way they behave seems like loving and caring. But then it turns into controlling your every movement. When I was fifteen and first dating him, I loved that. I felt great that he was so concerned about me. I loved it until it got to be that he'd keep me waiting for hours to go out, calling me every half hour to say that he was on his way. He'd tell me he'd pick me up at five, and then wouldn't turn up until nine o'clock, but he wanted to make sure that I didn't go anywhere or do anything except wait for him."

Since Judy had left him four years earlier, he has used their child as a way to remain in her life. Judy told how he would keep the child late on the days he had visitation rights. Then she would have to go and pick up the child at his house. He'd destroyed her new boyfriend's car, and threatened to kill her boyfriend if he didn't stop seeing her. So her recent boyfriend decided that she wasn't worth dying for, and left her.

Alcohol and drug abuse seem to be strong contributing factors for some batterers, although men often beat their partners without being drunk or high on drugs. It's easy to blame drugs and alcohol for many cases of battering women. And many observers do suggest that the women who are most abused or battered seem to have been beaten by men who were drunk or drinking. Drugs and alcohol can and do change the chemistry in the body and some people become more violent under their influence. But, several other professionals I met at these programs caution us not to assume that these men, if they stopped drinking, would end their abusive behavior. In fact, another myth is the belief (or hope) held by some women that if the men just stopped drinking, they would also stop abusing them. Several studies, including extensive research conducted by Lenore Walker, one of the foremost experts in the area of battered women, found about half of the beatings occurred when the men were under the influence of drugs or alcohol or both.

In the recent years, as with the increased use of cocaine and crack, the drugs generally accepted to provoke violence, men are even more abusive and highly dangerous.

Many of the men are not psychopaths, although one would assume that. Why else would they abuse people in their home, put the life of the mother of their children at risk, hurt the one they suppose to love? The definition of a psychopath is that he does not feel any remorse, does not know right from wrong. Many of these men can differentiate, they are sorry for their actions, and often, they shower the women with gifts afterward. According to some of the studies conducted by Angela Browne, and Lenore Walker, among others, many of these men are like the fictional character Dr. Jekyll, a kind, generous man transformed into the evil Mr. Hyde. These men are able to charm women, to show extreme love and concern, and then turn abusive.

NONVIOLENCE

NEGOTIATION AND FAIRNESS
Seeking mutually satisfying resolutions to conflict • accepting change • being willing to compromise.

NON-THREATENING BEHAVIOR
Talking and acting so that she feels safe and comfortable expressing herself and doing things.

ECONOMIC PARTNERSHIP
Making money decisions together • making sure both partners benefit from financial arrangements.

RESPECT
Listening to her non-judgmentally • being emotionally affirming and understanding • valuing opinions.

EQUALITY

SHARED RESPONSIBILITY
Mutually agreeing on a fair distribution of work • making family decisions together.

TRUST AND SUPPORT
Supporting her goals in life • respecting her right to her own feelings, friends, activities, and opinions.

RESPONSIBLE PARENTING
Sharing parental responsibilities • being a positive non-violent role model for the children.

HONESTY AND ACCOUNTABILITY
Accepting responsibility for self • acknowledging past use of violence • admitting being wrong • communicating openly and truthfully.

NONVIOLENCE

This Equality Wheel is used in educational groups for men who batter. Developed by the Duluth Domestic Abuse Intervention Project, of Duluth, Minnesota. the wheel is a starting point for discussion among the men.

This Power and Control Wheel is used by facilitators of educational groups for men who batter. The wheel helps the men to recognize which of their actions are abusive. The educational program has been developed by the Duluth Domestic Abuse Intervention Project.

These dynamics have been at the center of these relationships. While they exhibit personality disorders, like con artists, they engage a woman, gain her trust, and then seem to become another person. They are often very manipulative, but most are not sociopaths and, to outsiders, seem to live a normal life. We will further explore the core of the relationship of the battered women and their partners, in the following chapters. However, it is important to understand that while it seems hard to believe, these men are not monsters. They also do not abuse the women daily or all the time. It is the cycle of love, guilt, affection, and the abuse that is at the heart of the destructive relationship. "They are not monsters? Well, they seem to be," I added, as we discussed these men with a group of women and the program coordinator at a program designed for abused women.

"No. But they act like monsters, sometimes. But if we think of them as just monsters, then we are missing the point," added the program coordinator. During our conversations, they continued to stress that these men are not abusive all the time, that it is their cycle from extreme love and caring, their ability to feel guilt, their sense that they seem "normal" most of the time and that often these abusive relationships escalate over time, that is important to keep in mind. "If they were plain monsters, then so many women would not be in love with them."

Battered women claim that they feel guilty about splitting up the family and believe that leaving with the children would hurt the children. According to several surveys, some of the women who used their children as a reason for staying with an abuser, remained there long after the children had left home.

"Why do men batter their partners?" I asked everyone. Everyone gave me the same answer: "Because they can."

I heard that answer repeatedly from the women, the

counselors in the shelter, and the program counselors who work with the men. "That's it?" I asked.

One counselor who works with a program for abusers in New Jersey, expanded on the single phrase: "Men resort to violence because they want to control the women. But they beat them because they can get away with beating them. That's why they do it. They do not hit a boss, or a police officer who gives them a traffic ticket. They don't hit strangers on the street. They go home and they hit the person they're supposed to love."

Ellen Pence, director of the Domestic Abuse Intervention Project in Duluth, Minnesota, put it this way in a Time magazine interview.[2]

"A lot of people experience low impulse control, fear of abandonment, alcohol and drug addiction, all the characteristics of a batterer. However, the same guy is not beating up his boss." If a man were to beat his boss, he would be arrested. In other relationships, he simply would not get away with it."

This is the point every person I interviewed wanted to make. The batterer thinks that he can get away with hitting his wife and his children because he has done it for years and not been punished for it. For this reason many abuse counselors strongly feel that men must serve time for assault, whether they hurt a stranger or a partner. As long as they can get away with it, they will continue to do it.

"Your boss fires you. But you don't hit him. You go home and your wife burns the toast and you almost kill her." Charlotte Watson, an advocate for victims of domestic violence, uses this example to show why she doesn't believe a batterer is just violent by nature, or unable to control his temper. Why doesn't he hit the boss who, by firing him, may force him out on the street? He knows he has to control his anger and not kill the boss, because the law and society say that he cannot, and he will not get away with it. We must build the same kind of attitude about domestic violence. Men must no longer be able to beat a woman and get away with it.

I asked about the men's drinking patterns. "My husband would drink, but that was not the reason he hit me," said one battered wife. "He hit me because I came back late from the store, or I talked back to him. He was always sure that I would leave him. He had a constant fear that I would leave him."

There was bitter laughter as the other women agreed that the men seemed obsessed with the idea of being left, but never thought there was a problem with their leaving the women. The men seemed to think that was their right.

Many of the women also wanted to talk about the men's insecurity in regard to their own children or the woman's child from a previous relationship. When I first began talking to battered women, I had been amazed to meet several women with babies in shelters, and even a woman who was three months' pregnant. I thought only a truly insane man would hit a partner who was pregnant or had a small baby. But children trigger the fears that many of these men have of being left or pushed aside.

The men resent that the woman expresses affection for the baby instead of for them. They regard the baby as competing for the woman's time and attention. These men react in very immature ways. If the baby cries, the man finds that he needs something from the woman right then. He will want dinner served at the very moment that the baby is being fed. If the woman is busy putting the child to sleep, he wants to make love just then.

Some of the men had raped their partners just after the women had given birth to prove to themselves that the women still loved them. All the women who had children mentioned having major problems once the baby was born. It was as if the men were so threatened that they were unable to behave like adults, never mind as fathers.

Do the women see these men as crazy? Clearly these men are not healthy adults with normal fears and normal needs for attention and love.

As one woman said, "You would love him if you met him. To people outside, he was nice, he was in control, he seemed strong, and the type that we respect in our society. But he was also very moody, and at home you never knew what was bothering him. He could never just sit down and say, 'I had a bad day, I need to cuddle up with you.'"

These men seemed unable to vent their frustrations in a socially acceptable way. They could not show weakness in a way that is normal in close relationships, nor could they communicate well. When they got angry, they lashed out at the nearest target, the target that they felt would tolerate anything.

It is clear, also, that men who abuse women regularly view the women as children or as inferior to them. They look upon the women as their property living in their homes. The men are the ones who make all the decisions about their lives. There is no equality in the relationship.

After listening to so many sad and awful stories of abuse, I asked the women the obvious question, "Why didn't you leave?" Almost all of them wanted to answer.

"You don't understand. It's not as if they beat you all the time," responded a rather tough-sounding woman who had spent five years with an abusive man who had fathered one of her children. When he came home one day, and asked if someone had called, she gave him a flip answer, "I ain't your secretary." That resulted in a rage. At the same time, he was openly dating another woman.

Now, she had moved out — for the third time. She said that sometimes it was a year between the beatings, and that things were good between them for long periods of time. "I had almost forgotten the last time he hit me." She added, "Things were fine; we argued and fought, but who doesn't?" was her attitude.

"The first time he hits you is when you should leave," was the advice that these women seemed to agree on — although they had not followed their own suggestion. The other advice they wanted to share was that women should refuse to accept joking around and hitting that's supposed to be "play." They agreed that the "play " hitting eventually became real abuse.

After years of abuse, particularly when it escalated, the women did hit back and tried to defend themselves by kicking, biting, and whatever means they could use. This only led to more punches. The men reacted as if this were a game they were playing and they needed to prove they were stronger and in control. In fact, some beatings proved fatal when the women responded with greater violence and the men felt that they had to strike the last blow.

Sometimes the attacks lasted only a few minutes, but the pain they caused could extend over weeks. Following the hostility, the men would bring gifts and make promises that it would never happen again. At times, the women wanted to forgive and did, athough they didn't forget the pain.

"Could you get someone here now. . . . He's back. Please!" This could have been a call made by any of the women in this book, or by one or the 200,000 victims of domestic violence each year. The only thing that made this call to the police so sensational was the identity of the caller. This is the call that O. J. Simpson's ex-wife Nicole made months before she was killed. Whatever the outcome in the murder trial of O. J. Simpson, the fact that he had abused his ex-wife is a matter of record. In 1989 he was charged, pleaded no contest, and paid a $700 fine for an attack that required hospital treatment.

It is shocking that a man who is so successful, wealthy, handsome, respected and popular, used to hit his wife. But it is not only men who have low self-esteem, are uneducated, poor, unemployed, or on drugs who abuse women. This is a problem that can affect every relationship when the man feels that he must control his partner and own her, and when jealousy becomes an obsession. These relationships sometimes become abusive and violent.

Since the revelations about O. J. Simpson became public, calls to domestic violence hot lines have increased dramatically, in some places by 80 percent. Many women were calling for the first time. Perhaps this tragic incident can help to bring about a change in attitude. We must acknowledge that domestic violence can happen among every family, even among people who seem to have it all.

COUNSELING PROGRAMS
FOR ABUSIVE MEN

In preparing for this book I was able to talk to many women. Most were in shelters or had left the shelters to live on their own. Most were eager to tell me their stories, and to talk openly about their relationships. Information about the men came mostly from these women and from counselors who had worked with both the men and the women in the programs. These counseling programs, usually mandated by the court when the men are arrested for domestic violence, work to help men understand their behavior toward the women, their need to dominate, and their unhealthy view of their partners. Unfortunately, abusers join these programs only when ordered to do so by courts (in place of prison terms) or when pressured by the women who threaten to leave them unless they attend. Most of the women who had the courage to insist that the men attend group therapy sessions for abusive men had already been in a shelter, or had left the relationship at least once before.

I must add, sadly, that many of the women had little faith in these programs. "Of course, he went for group sessions for six weeks instead of jail, wouldn't you?" responded one woman. She had pressed charges for assault, and had moved out of her apartment and been referred to a shelter by the Victim Services Society, an organization that provides various types of assistance to battered women in New York City. Instead of a jail term, her abuser was given probation and ordered to attend weekly group meetings for six weeks, in the hope that he would change his behavior toward his partner. She wasn't optimistic; therefore, she decided to file for divorce. This man had dominated her for six years and had hit her for five of those years.

"What is six weeks going to do for a man who thinks that it is his own business what he does with his wife?" many battered wives ask. The counselors in a program for men gave only limited encouragement. They said that change was unlikely unless the men attended the program because the men themselves wanted to change their behavior. The men must recognize that what they had done was dangerous to the family and hurtful to all involved.

"Only other men can get abusive men to stop hurting their partners," said one counselor. The problem seems rooted in an attitude that these men share — that they are stronger and should dominate, and that it is their right to teach their women a lesson by hitting them or putting them in place.

MACHO MALE ATTITUDES
Men often justify this type of behavior in conversations like, "That bitch was really acting up. I had to take care of her before she really got out of line and forgot who I am."

And the other man responds, "I know, I have to do that too once in a while, so she remembers who is in charge and who she's talking to. I am the man in this house."

These men may spend a lot of time with other men, often choosing companions who condone abusive behavior, and think that it is normal to hit their women. Some men may never tell anyone what they do at home. Other men brag about their behavior, finding in it a sense of power and a boost for their self-image that is a substitute for real power or achievement.

These men tend to blame others for problems, and do not accept responsibility for anything. Unlike most people, they can't admit that they mishandled a situation or that they were disappointed about something. Instead, some drown their sorrows in drugs or alcohol, and then take out their frustration by blaming their partner.

Many of these men have learned this behavior in the course of their upbringing. They have seen in their families that aggression is the way to settle arguments and deal with pain, frustration, and anger. Society must educate everyone that there are ways to argue and disagree without resorting to violence.

Some observers say that the men and the women in abusive relationships have a lot in common, although their behavior is different. Because both the man and the woman have low self-esteem, they both need to hold on to each other in the beginning. As time passes, however, the relationship becomes more skewed and perhaps the women start to break away. The men feel inadequate, and try to prove their masculinity by controlling their women by force.

Why do men batter? They batter for many reasons. For one thing, society tolerates their actions. Society must get across the message that abusive behavior "is not OK." We don't let people smoke in the subways or shoot drugs in the streets. Men should not be able to break a partner's or child's jaw, and go on to the next day as if nothing happened. Something did happen. They caused damage and pain that will be in their victims' lives forever.

CHAPTER EIGHT

WOMEN WHO KILL

Self-defense is recognized by the courts as a legitimate defense. But with domestic violence, self-defense is rarely accepted in cases in which women are accused of murdering their partners.

According to Angela Browne, in *When Battered Women Kill*, the number of women who will be killed by their abusers is far greater than the number of abusers who will be killed by their victims. In 1991, 1,320 abused women were killed. Fewer than half that number of women — 622 — killed their abuser.[1] Yet the women received average sentences of fifteen to twenty years while the men's sentences averaged two to six years, according to the Battered Women's Justice Center of Pace University.[2]

Who are these women who resort to killing their partners? In one survey conducted by Angela Browne, the women ranged in age from nineteen through fifty-eight, and they had an average of two children. Sixty-six percent of the women were white, 22 percent were black, and 12 percent Latino.

Almost 50 percent had working-class backgrounds, about 25 percent had low incomes, and another 25 percent were middle class. Only about 5 percent were from the upper economic group, which may be due to the fact that women with greater financial resources have more options.[3]

The women were relatively well educated. Nearly three-quarters had finished high school, and nearly a quarter had attended college. Slightly fewer than half the women were employed, in full- or part-time jobs.

The women who had committed homicide had been involved with the men almost nine years, and 80 percent were married to their abusers. These women were often involved with men from a lower social class than themselves. A smaller percentage of the men had finished high school — only 60 percent, as opposed to 71 percent of the women. About half of the men worked, which is about the same figure for the women.

Browne's research indicated that the severity and frequency of the abuse in the battering relationships was a significant factor that led to the homicides. The frequency of abusive incidents was higher in the homicide group than in a control group of abused women who did not kill their abusers. Sixty-three percent reported being abused more than once a month, 13 percent reported weekly abuse, and about 40 percent of the women in the homicide group reported being abused more than once a week. These figures are considerably higher than those for the women in the control group.[4]

Over 80 percent of the women in the homicide group stated that the abuse became worse over time. Most significantly, in the homicide group the women had become convinced that their partners would kill them, and the abusers did make frequent threats to kill them.

Another difference between the two groups of women relates to the children. In the homicide group, over 70 percent of the children were physically and sexually abused by their mother's abuser. In the group of women who did not resort to killing the abuser, 50 percent of the children experienced physical or sexual abuse, or both.

A third significant difference between these two groups is the impact of drugs and alcohol on the men.

Most researchers and domestic-violence workers claim that alcohol and drugs should not be blamed for the injury that abusive men inflict on their families. Nevertheless, it is a factor. Among abusive men in the control group, 40 percent became intoxicated from alcohol every day. That is well above the average in society.

Among the men who were killed by their victims, 79 percent were intoxicated every day by the end of the relationship. Women reported that when the men were drinking, they were most violently abusive. As time went on, the men also drank more often, leading to even more frequent abuse.

Drug use was also much higher among the men in this group. About 30 percent used drugs on a daily or near daily basis, while among the abusive men in the control group, 8 percent abused drugs daily.[5]

The women used guns against their abusers in 80 percent of the cases, often the same one that the abuser had threatened to use against them. Almost all the women in Browne's group stated that they had tried to leave the relationship. Some had left and then returned. They had feared that leaving would result in their death.

Charles Ewing, a researcher on domestic abuse, also compared 100 battered women who had killed their partners with 100 battered women who hadn't taken that final step.[6] According to his study, women who resorted to violence were usually the most isolated and the most badly beaten. Corroborating Browne's findings, he found their partners were drug and alcohol abusers and their children had been abused. The common threads connecting women who killed their abusers were the circumstances in which they lived, not homicidal tendencies. According to Ewing, they were not pathological; they were the women living with the worst abuse.

From these and other researchers' work we can create a profile of the women who kill their abusers. For the most part, they have no criminal records and have not previously committed crimes. Many lived through years of abuse and reached their breaking points when they learned their children were also being abused.

But many women do not kill their partners at the time of abuse. Often they wait and kill the men when the men are least expecting an attack. This makes it difficult for the women to claim they acted in self-defense. One expert supports a self-defense plea in this way: "Do we have to wait until his hand is on her throat before she can retaliate? If he says, 'I am going to kill you tomorrow' does she have to wait until tomorrow arrives before she defends herself?"

If a stranger attacks you with a gun, threatening to kill you and you struggle with him and kill him with a broken bottle or fight him for the gun and shoot him, self-defense can seem like a clear argument. A domestic-violence case can be less clear. A woman has lived with an abuser for years, and the abuse gets increasingly worse, until she claims she fears for her life. She has called the police in the past but that only led to more beatings. One night — not in the heat of an abuse attack, but as he sleeps — she gets his gun and shoots him. Should this woman also be able to claim that she killed in self-defense? What about the cases in which a woman hires someone else to kill her abuser? How can she then claim self-defense?

The case of Rita Collins was widely reported. She had killed her husband after what she claimed was a lifetime of abuse. In interviews on several television programs and in Time magazine, she described her husband John, who was a military recruiter, as "a solid man who had a way with words." He had verbally abused her, kicked her, threatened her with knives, and punched her in the stomach. Navy doctors had treated her for injuries in her neck and arm.

After the couple retired, they bought a house in Florida. She filed for divorce, got a restraining order, filed an assault-and-battery charge against him, and then forced him out of the house. But night after night, he came to the house, banging on the windows, trying to break down the doors. According to Mrs. Collins, the police seemed unable to do anything and had suggested that she get a gun. Finally, she did get a gun and killed her husband with that gun after he lunged at her with a knife, although she claims to remember nothing about pulling the trigger. She was found guilty of second-degree murder. Collins is still in prison. She was denied clemency, even though many of her friends, her doctor, and her minister had all testified that she had suffered violence in her marriage.

The "battered women's syndrome" is the term used to describe the usual defense for women who, after years of abuse, turn on their abusers. The lives of these battered women who have killed follow a similar pattern. They believed that their abuse would never end and many committed the act at a moment of opportunity, rather than during actual abuse. Many of them had thought about killing their abuser, but they had never believed they would actually do it. They also were surprised by their courage in facing their abuser and often said they did not mean to kill him. Some committed the act after their children were abused and said that while they could endure their own abuse, they could no longer stand seeing their children hurt.

What should the legal system do about these cases? The governor of Ohio, Richard Celeste, pardoned twenty-seven women in 1990, citing battered women's syndrome as defense. "They had not had the opportunity for a fair trial because vitally important evidence affecting their circumstances and the terrible things done to them was not presented to the jury."[7]

While other governors did not follow his example of clemency, Governor Celeste created a public awareness of the desperation of battered women.

Some critics are afraid that it will become too easy for any woman to use the plea of the battered woman. Supporters claim that this concern is unwarranted and point out that, in many cases, women plead guilty to lesser charges to avoid a jury trial. Why does the woman plea-bargain? The woman fears that the jury would not be able to understand her plight or how someone could endure years of abuse and then — not in a moment of imminent danger — kill her tormentor.

Other women plea-bargain because they do not have the funds for private lawyers, or are represented by public defenders who lack the time or the experience to represent them properly. To demonstrate the truth of this last point, 40 percent of the first convictions of the women who have killed their abusers have been reversed on appeal.[8]

As we noted earlier, North Carolina in 1874 was the first state to limit a man's right to beat his wife. But these enlightened lawmakers also stated that unless the man was beating his wife to death, "It is better to draw the curtain, shut out the public gaze and leave the parties to forget and forgive."[9]

Some 120 years later, society still does not treat domestic violence seriously, considering the danger it poses to the women. According to a Boston Bar Association study, aggravated assault against a stranger is considered a felony, but the same assault committed at home is judged only a misdemeanor. Furthermore, in 1990, the author of a gender bias study commissioned by the Florida Supreme Court reported that police seldom arrest, even when there are injuries serious enough to require hospitalization of the victim. According to the Bureau of Justice Statistics' National Crime Survey, one–third of the domestic violence assaults committed against women would be considered felonies in most states, if the incident occurred outside the home.[10]

Some advocates for domestic violence victims ask, What choice does a battered woman really have? Finding no support in the justice system, alone, afraid, desperate, what can she do but to try to free herself from her abuser. But other people, who are less compassionate, argue that there are appropriate legal ways to deal with marital problems, and a gun is never the answer to these problems.

While no one can possibly suggest that a woman should resort to violence, or that killing an abuser is an acceptable way to solve the problem, supporters of battered women say that violent husbands and fathers and partners should be treated as criminals. If they are not arrested, tried, or jailed for their abuse, society gives them license to continue to beat women and children. Society has failed to teach that their behavior is unacceptable.

The state of Minnesota has been a leader in facing this problem of domestic violence. In 1981 Duluth, Minnesota, became the first American city to require mandatory arrests in domestic violence cases. Since that time, about half the states have instituted similar guidelines. This means that even if a victim does not press charges, the police are obliged to arrest an abuser if they see evidence of abuse. Now prosecutors no longer drop the charges or accept a plea bargain to a lesser charge, and some of the men actually do jail time. The police are trained, also, to arrest abusers rather than talk to them, and thus the police stop further abuse.

In Jacksonville, Florida, the introduction of new procedures helped raise the number of arrests of abusers from 25 percent to 40 percent. This sends a strong message. The men are shown that their behavior is no longer acceptable, and the women now can hope that their calls to the police will be taken seriously. For the children, while it is troubling for them to see their father or guardian arrested, they are also given the message that violence at home is not acceptable and that it is not the way to resolve anger.

In Minnesota, better training is provided for emergency room workers, judges, and other professionals in handling domestic violence incidents. Minnesota also has rehabilitation programs for the men. Starting from the assumption that battering is a behavior that the men learned — probably in their homes while growing up — these programs teach the men to redirect their anger and frustration and release it in ways other than beating their wives.

If we are to find alternatives to women killing their abusive men, the police must improve their handling of the abused women. The courts must send a strong message that they will treat these cases seriously and not as disorderly conduct cases, as usually was the case in the past. There must be punishment to fit the crime.

Furthermore, programs must be created that will change men's behavior. Perhaps as a result of such efforts, the legal system will be able to deal with domestic problems, and no battered woman will feel compelled to take the law into her own hands. Then the debate between those who seek clemency for the women and those who want the violent acts treated as crimes will be resolved. For now, the Minnesota model is one that many counselors hope other states will copy.

CHAPTER NINE

SHELTERS FOR BATTERED WOMEN

Before visiting one shelter for battered women in Westchester County, I was instructed to look for a house without a number and with an electric surveillance camera on the porch. The house looked ordinary in other ways, but I couldn't enter it without providing the pre-arranged signal that I was indeed the person they were expecting.

At another shelter, they would agree to let me visit only if they could drive me there from their offices. I discovered later that, after an extensive detour, they had taken me around the block to the back of the same building. Most domestic-violence centers never gave me permission to visit or stay.

"Is safety really such a serious issue?" I asked one of the directors.

"Are you kidding?" she responded. "These women are fleeing for their lives. They are hiding from their partners, who might kill them if they knew where to find them. Remember, 75 percent of the women who are killed by their partners are killed when they try to leave."

So it is no wonder that these places are surrounded by the tightest security, and I was made to promise never to reveal where any of them are located.

The first shelter for battered women was started by a group of women from Al–Anon in Pasadena,

California, for families of alcoholics in 1965. Since then shelters have been set up throughout the world, from India to Canada.[1]

In the United States in the 1990s, there are about 1,500 shelters that operate as refuges for battered women. Shelters have been opened by feminists, by women who were abused themselves, and by women connected to religous organizations. Groups such as the National Organization of Women, which are concerned about women's rights, have raised money for shelters and hot lines for battered women.

Many of the shelters started as small places of refuge, with a few beds for emergency shelter. Some twenty years later, shelters have become a part of our society. They are funded by local governments, federal programs, social agencies, and private donations.

Most safe houses are small, with less than a hundred beds and accommodate women and children in a communal environment. The staff is usually comprised of women who are interested in the general welfare of other women. Some are social workers and counselors. In most places, the shelters are maintained by the abused women, who share the cooking, the cleaning, and the house chores, while the staff helps with housing, group counseling, and the paperwork required by the government bureaucracy. The staff helps the women get on welfare while at the shelter, finds tutoring for the children if they cannot attend school, and arranges for a free attorney for women who need legal representation.

The shelters' services encompass a hot line for battered women, support groups and advocacy counseling for women, and an educational component to teach nonviolent conflict resolution in local schools.

These shelters are modest yet homey. Each woman is offered a separate bedroom, which she shares with her children, and a communal dining room, where she may eat dinner with others. Some women stay a few nights, some a few weeks, and some up to three months. Some come with only the clothes on their back, and some come and stay until the court order for protection is served. Their stays generally last a month or longer, while they look for a place of their own.

"How do the women find these shelters?" I asked. The director of one of the domestic violence programs explained, "They usually call in through the hot line or are referred by a police officer, or if they've had to go into the emergency room of a hospital, the staff social worker may suggest that they come into the shelter."

The hot line phone number is listed. Some of the women find the number through the operator and other women who are not referred by a police officer or social worker are often referred by a friend.

I found that the population in shelters changes all the time. In any given month, one may meet women of many different backgrounds, although they tell similar stories. Most of the experts in this field, usually social workers, counselors, feminists, or psychologists, insist that domestic violence cuts across all ethnic and economic lines. However, most of the people in shelters tend to be women from lower economic backgrounds, because they lack easy access to private doctors or therapists or lawyers who can help women in crisis. Furthermore, a woman who can pay for a hotel room may hide there rather than in a shelter where her situation is no longer private. But those who work at the shelters say that the shelters are not used only by impoverished women.

Usually, when a woman goes to a shelter for the first time, she will return home. It takes a woman several tries before her leave is permanent. As one program director explained, "The first time the women go back because they still love the man, he is their Prince Charming. Ironically, we are not talking about some monster that no one can love. This guy is not always an abuser. They try to forget about the incident — the black eye or the bruises — and when he swears that it will never happen again, they try to believe him. Usually, the child wants to go back to school and to old friends, so there is a lot of pressure on her to return. Her partner sweet-talks her into going back."

It may be months or years before the next time that she returns to the shelter. This time she may leave with no intention of returning.

A coordinator of a shelter program located in Connecticut remarked, "Women have always been charged with the emotional well-being of the family. While men are supposed to be the breadwinners, women are supposed to take care of the home. So it is the woman's fault if there is something wrong with the marriage. The men reinforce this belief by constantly telling them that they hit them for their own good, or because they did or did not do something.

"The men never take responsibility for their actions, blaming it on the women. Then they may go to the woman's family, and her mother may also try to keep her from breaking up the family, or her priest may say 'Go home and try a little harder,' so leaving is a hard path. And they keep hoping that the abuse will stop. The one thing that I always try to tell people who interview me or ask about domestic violence — the women may keep hoping, but the abuse never stops."[2]

It takes about five to seven tries before the woman leaves the relationship for good, but every time a woman leaves, she is moving closer to the final exit. Everyone stressed the difficulty that the women faced in leaving their partners.

In the shelter, the women and some children can have a few days to collect themselves before they sort out what course of action they will take. These shelters offer help and information, but try not to decide for a woman what she should do: whether she should return home, leave, get divorced, or take some other action. The shelter's staff will stress to the women that the abuse will probably not stop unless they do something; however, they strongly believe that these women have been under the control of a partner and must now make their own decisions.

These shelters offer another new element. Most of the women have been isolated and have been living in fear of their partner and unable to discuss with anyone what was happening to them at home. This is the first time they see other women in similar circumstances. They can share stories and feel that they are no longer alone. Others feel for the first time that there may be an end in sight to their abuse, and some feel the courage to work to change their predicament.

Many of the women gain support from the others. They can see the similarities in their lives and recognize how undeserved their own treatment was. They gain some hope that they can make it without their partner, or that they may be able to escape their fate at home.

Among the women I met, some would return home, after years of severe abuse, for fear that they would be killed. Some would leave the shelter with court orders of protection taken out against their partner. Other women laughed at the idea of protection from the court.

One of the women voiced her feelings: "Those court orders don't do anything. You must be kidding. The man I live with is not going to care about that piece of paper. He said that he will kill my children, and I believe him." Her children were sitting next to her nodding their heads in agreement.

But some of the women in shelters were trying to resolve their life with the abuser in a different way. Those who had experienced severe and ongoing physical abuse and who had already attempted many escapes now felt protected while in the shelter, for the first time in many years.

They were using the days or weeks in the shelter to get all the legal support for permanent protection from their abuser. Some started divorce procedures, while others pressed criminal charges against the men. The legal assistance, a vitally important service that many of the shelters provide, along with the counseling and psychological support of the social workers and the other women, made them feel that while still afraid, they were able to take their life into their own hands.

Some women meet in shelters and move away from the old area to set up homes together, sharing child care and other household duties, so they can begin new lives.

The program coordinator for a domestic-violence shelter located in an office building in Connecticut, commented on how these women actually change their psychological perspective while in the shelter. "It's amazing. When the women first come here they don't go out. They're afraid to go to the park for fear that the men will find them here, although everyone needs a pass to get in these shelter doors and the office building has a receptionist downstairs and several mazes and hallways and doors to get through in order to reach the area of the shelter. A few weeks later, they go out to the park and even further, yet the reality is probably the same. The men could easily find them if they were tracking them. Yet the women seem to develop a little more confidence, or are less afraid of the consequences."

Understandably, when the women first come in, most are totally traumatized from their experiences. They sit quietly and do not want to talk, while the women who have been in the shelter for a few weeks are often eager and happy to share their stories. Often they arrive with their children in the middle of the night or on a weekend, bruised from the abuse. It is painful to see them. At first they are not sure what to expect. While the abuse is fresh on their bodies and in their minds, they are sure that they will never go back and also are afraid that they will be killed.

In material terms, the shelters provide only the bare basics: a roof, food, and safety. But more significantly, a shelter is a place where the abused women can share their stories and their lives, and gain the strength to try to go on with their life. For many, the physical pain may have subsided, but not the anger or sadness about their treatment and the loss of their love. A shelter is a place where they can pause, a place where they feel secure and share their histories, and receive counseling. Here they can begin to see that they can live without the men.

The women who go back home, take with them a new perspective about the nature of their relationship. One woman who had been physically hurt for years returned home after a brief stay at the shelter. She returns to the shelter for regular support-group sessions. At one meeting she reported, with a smile, "Last night, he called me a bitch and poked me with his finger. I looked at him calmly and said 'Take your damn finger away from my shoulder or I'll walk out of here this minute. I mean it.' You know, he moved back, mumbled something, and walked out of the room."

The counselor pointed out to me that this women had been severely abused for years and now, after being a part of the shelter and listening to other women, she could face her abuser and say, "Stop it."

Even the women who choose to return to live with their men seem to have a better sense of themselves and their options. And they are armed with a surer sense that men cannot just abuse them. They can fight back, and some can start new lives without the hurt. Also, while the women talk a lot about revenge and how they want to kill their abusers, they begin to see that violence is not the solution to their problems.

The stories I heard in the shelters were amazingly similar, and many of the characteristics of the men also seemed identical. The men started out as loving and charming and the women became dependent on them for everything. As the women became increasingly isolated and dominated psychologically and physically, they believed that they were responsible for the beatings and that they deserved the abuse.

Some of the women were manipulated into believing that the abuse and the beatings were a sign the men really cared about them and loved them. The men would say "If I didn't care about you, baby, I wouldn't even bother with you, or take the time to tell you things and get you into line." Some parents may hit a child's hand to train the child to stay away from the oven. They say, "I am going to hit you if you do that again. Now, you'll remember not to do that again." The same method is used by the men; they treat the women like children and tell them hitting is a sign of caring, and is intended to teach them something.

During a group session with five women in a shelter, two said they had never gone to the police. Another had been severely beaten by a former boyfriend despite the fact that she had a court order of protection. The police had claimed they could not find him but when she went to pick up her child at school, he was there. She asked the cop on the corner to serve him with the paper, but he responded, "I'll watch you while you give it to him." That night, the boyfriend came to her house and he found out that she was seeing a new man and beat her brutally in her mother's hallway.

She was placed in a shelter out of town, but she knows he is still on the streets, and lives near her mother's house. "It kills me to be in here. The other day I went back to see my mother. I didn't tell her that I was coming. She opened the door and was so scared that she just wanted me out of there. This is no way to live."

Her ten-year-old son was asked if he wanted to join in our group session. His mother encouraged him to go outside. "Why don't you go out to the backyard with the other kids and play. This will be boring." But he said he wanted to stay. He listened for a while, but when we talked about his mother being severely beaten by his father — someone he continued to visit — he left quickly.

His mother, twenty-nine years old and very determined, quietly said, "He feels very bad because he told his father about my boyfriend. He's scared to death now, and never wants to see his father again. Beyond the pain or getting hit, what is so sad is that we were together so long. He was my first best friend and we cared about each other."

All the women nodded their heads. They had loved these men at one time. They all lamented that this part of them had died. They would never love this way again. Now they concentrate on resolving their problems, if for no other reason than for the sake of their children.

THE CHILDREN

Since most of the shelters house many of the women's children, the noise level and the tension is often high, particularly when the house is nearly full. The children tend to be hyperactive. They are excited and afraid because they are in a new environment, in hiding, and cannot do the things they would like. They cannot go to the movies or visit friends or make some phone calls, because they cannot reveal where they are. This is difficult for many of them because they don't understand why they can't talk to their friends or a favorite uncle or even their father. They are uncertain about how long they will be in these homes, when and if they are going back to school, and when they will be able to return to their old life. As violent as it may have been, it is the one that they know.

Other children, particularly the older ones who have also been physically abused, have mixed feelings. "Do you want to go back home?" I asked an eleven-year-old. "Yes. I just want my mother and stepfather to stop fighting and hitting. I can't stand that, and sometimes I get hit because they got into a fight and they take it out on me for something small that I did. But, yeah, I want to go back and play with my toys, and talk to my friends, see my cousin, and hang out. I'm bored here."

But the uncertainty of the future is also very scary for many of the children. Where will they go? Will they see anyone they used to know? While some of the children can understand that they and their mother are in danger, some wonder how come they are suddenly in danger, when they have been living in the midst of brutal fighting for years.

One woman came into the shelter during a weekend, bringing her three teenage sons. This shelter was unusual in that it accepts most women, even those with teenage children, or with a drug or alcohol problem, as long as they do not abuse drugs or alcohol while in the facility and the children are not too disruptive for the rest of the residents. When I saw her, she was in a daze. She had come to the shelter less than twenty-four hours before, having traveled from another town at the suggestion of the police, and terrified that her boyfriend was going to kill her children.

One of the boys was wearing a University of Pennsylvania T-shirt he had pulled from the shelter's boxes of clothing that are kept ready for those who arrive with nothing but the clothes on their back. He said that he too was a writer. "What type of things do you write?" I asked. "Oh, murder stories." He shrugged. "I like to write about mass murderers."

Later he added that he read only on a first-grade level, although he was in the seventh grade, because he had a learning disability. His older brother, who was sixteen and at least 50 pounds overweight, had the same problem. The damage that the years of abuse had wrought on their lives was apparent. The children were already violent with each other, with significant learning disabilities, and years behind in school. Though unable to write, one wanted to write about mass murderers.

The director, Mary Beth, said, "All the children have been abused, whether or not they were also physically the target of the abuse. Living in the fear and the violence that they witness or know about is abusive to all children. Many of them have problems in school, serious learning disabilities, emotional and behavioral problems, scars that stay with them forever. Violence becomes the norm for them in resolving conflict. So the next generation of abusers is in the making."

The children in general were hyperactive. They have become used to uncertainty and violence at home, and often blame themselves for the arguments between the adults. Often, their homes consisted of a mother and a stepfather, and they believed that their presence contributed to the tension and fighting at home. Some of the children told me that they wanted to run away from home, and some actually had run away and returned. Some were very withdrawn, yet others liked to talk and were curious about why I was writing a book about battered women. They assumed that I was one of those women, too.

"So, what happened with you?" asked one young boy. "I was never battered, but I hope to write about other women's experiences," I said. He looked a bit puzzled and added, "My mother wasn't battered either. She and her boyfriend just used to fight a lot and sometimes my mother would yell back at him or just not do what he said, and he would throw something or hit her. Sometimes it got worse and then they'd get into a fight. I'd run into my room and turn the TV on loud. I just couldn't stand it. But I hope that they work it out."

According to his mother, the situation was much worse than her son knew because she tried to protect him and sent him to camp in the summer or to her mother's, so he would not hear the way her boyfriend talked to her. She feared her son would grow to disrespect her. She added, "It's amazing how much of my energy was spent for years, preparing for the abuse, handling the abuse, protecting myself from getting killed, sweet-talking him into stopping the violence, or trying to anticipate what would trigger an explosion, and trying to protect the children from the abuse. Now, for the first time, I feel as if a ton of bricks has been lifted and I can think of myself and a future, because I don't live in fear every day, hoping that he will not go off on me, not abuse me, shout and yell at me, tell me how stupid I was, how useless, how I was nothing without him, and constantly putting me down. If only for a few weeks, I feel wonderful."

According to Superintendent Lord, of Bedford Hills correctional facility, the maximum-security prison for women in New York State, the shelters are responsible for the fact that there are fewer women in prison for fatally killing their abuser.

These shelters are not meant to be the answer for the long term, since most of them have a maximum stay of a few months. But that time gives the women a breather. They can get help for their children, and many find new courage to face their future, without the sense of helplessness and defeat they had lived with for years. Now, after time spent in the shelter, many can begin a new life. They can return for the weekly group sessions, and at least they know that there is a place where they can turn to for help. The isolation is over.

CHAPTER TEN

CONCLUSION

"If you believe all those stories women tell you about being abused, then you'll believe anything." That was a comment from a male cabdriver who drove me to the train station from a suburban shelter for abused women I had just visited. He seemed to know the purpose of the house, even though it fit unobtrusively into the neighborhood of small, well-kept, modest houses, with children playing on the streets.

"Why, you don't believe that they're victims of abuse?" I asked during our three-minute ride.

"You must be kidding. These women are just living off the system. Sure, a man and a woman can have a fight and someone gets hit sometimes. But women hit men, too."

As I rode on the train to New York City, I thought about his view. Yes, it is true. There were questions as to whether they were all victims. The women also disagreed about whether they viewed themselves as abused. Some had just wanted to get away from the "crazy man" they loved before somebody got killed.

But one fact still stuck in my mind. Ninety-five percent of domestic violence consists of abuse committed by men against women. Women are the ones who end up in emergency rooms. They are the ones who get hurt. Even when women fight back, they are not strong enough to inflict the same injuries the men are capable of inflicting on them.

Domestic violence is a tragedy for all involved, and especially the children who grow up with continual violence as the model for their behavior. No wonder they are violent in school, in the playground, with their friends, and in later years with their girlfriends and wives. Domestic violence is at the heart of many of the problems that we face as a society. Children who come from abusive homes, children who grow up with violence as part of the climate at home, think that this behavior is what happens in all homes.

Domestic violence is about many things: love, abuse, control of women, the legal system, unequal treatment of women in this society, and finally, the human tragedy when love has gone sour, yet no one knows how to end the relationship without inflicting scars for life. The violence is a part of life that neither the women, nor the children, nor the men can ever really forget.

As I talked with battered women, I learned, first, to really understand the answer to the question everyone asks: "Why don't women just leave?" At one evening session at a women's shelter the women — enjoying a new self-confidence, developed through their bonding with women of similar experiences — declared that none of them would ever return to what they had left behind.

One woman insisted that as soon as a man puts a hand on you, that's the time to leave. Yet she had stayed with a man for five years — a man who repeatedly hit her and punched her. Although she says that she fought back, her attempts had been futile against the fury of his punches. Until now, she had not left him because, as she put it, "I was not through with him" — meaning, she still loved him and could not leave him, even though he abused her. The dynamics of these relationships —

the love that the men give when they are not abusive, the women's love in return, the men's dominant need of control and the fear their behavior creates — make for complicated relationships.

I have presented these women's stories to shed light on domestic violence. We need to understand how these relationships evolve, and how the women tolerate years of abuse, in order to see what society can do to help them. Their children who are growing up in violent environments must receive help in order to prevent the cycle from being repeated in the next generation.

If we accept the facts that 4 million women are abused yearly and that more women miscarry due to physical abuse than to medical problems, then we can dispense with the myth that domestic violence is rare and only happens among the mentally ill or among alcohol and drug abusers.

I found that the women were not all docile or helpless, although many of them were ignorant of their rights. Many of the women were immigrants and seemed the most vulnerable. Some had no idea that their babies could be taken away from them if they had not secured custody rights. They had little knowledge of protection laws governing domestic violence, and they had a real fear of calling the police. Minority women, women on welfare, and women who were immigrants were reluctant to go to court, were afraid to press charges, and were convinced that their abusers would kill them if they took action.

It is amazing how domestic violence affected everyone in the family. The women had become increasingly less productive, the men had become more violent, and the children were scarred emotionally. Everyone had been hurt. No one was a winner in this situation. The children had no parents, and the parents had no support or love at home.

Domestic violence is not a private matter. We cannot — as the law of 1874 in North Carolina suggested — draw the curtains, and forgive and forget. A society must intervene. We must recognize that the entire family is abused, and the children will grow up to become the next generation of abusers. They will not know anything else. They will believe that violence is what you do to those you supposedly love. We must help fight the vicious cycle. Domestic violence is not a women's issue, it is a human issue. It is a family problem, one that we all need to work to end.

If you are living in a house with abuse, know that there is help. The police are mandated to stop the abuse. Women need to know that they can get help, that there are shelters and laws to protect them. If we know someone who is being abused, we can help them with information. If the courts crack down on the abusers, if the programs help men channel their anger away from violence, if we protect the women and children, if we can interrupt the cycle of violence, we may have some hope for the next generation. Perhaps then we can end the sad legacy of pain.

APPENDIX ONE:

FACTS ABOUT BATTERING

- 95 percent of all victims are women.
- Approximately 4 million women are battered annually.
- Battering is the single major cause of injury to women, exceeding rapes, muggings, and auto accidents combined.
- Women are seven times as likely to resort to violence in self-defense.
- Three out of five women will be battered at least once in their lifetime.
- Four thousand women are killed by their partners each year.
- Battering occurs in every class, religion, race, educational level, and cultural group.
- Abuse escalates over time, often starting as verbal attacks, erupting into violence and becoming increasingly violent.
- Every fifteen seconds, a woman is beaten.

APPENDIX TWO:

MYTHS ABOUT BATTERING

Most people, whether or not they realize it, have attitudes and beliefs about battering that are based on myths. Myths are false statements that most people think are true. The following statements are myths that you, your family, your friends, even your doctor or minister or lawyer might believe.

MYTHS ABOUT
BATTERED WOMEN:

• Battered women are masochistic; they like being beaten.

• Only black or Hispanic women are battered.

• Battered women deserve to be beaten; they provoke it.

• Middle class and rich women are never battered.

• If a battered woman wanted to leave, she would get plenty of help to do so.

MYTHS ABOUT
BATTERERS:

• Drinking causes men to batter.

• A batterer must also beat his children.

• God-fearing men don't batter.

- Batterers are never loving; they are mean and violent all of the time.
- Educated professional men don't batter.
- Batterers are violent with many other people, such as co-workers and friends.

APPENDIX THREE:

THE DULUTH DOMESTIC ABUSE INTERVENTION PROJECT

The Duluth Domestic Abuse Intervention Project, of the Minnesota Program Development, Inc., conducts seminars and publishes training materials for people who work with domestic-abuse victims: shelter advocates, police, prosecutors, judges, probation officers, counselors and group facilitators, Native American service providers, and human service providers. The National Training Project presents week-long institutes several times a year, to which communities send several policymakers who will organize a coordinated response to domestic assault cases. The Duluth Project also publishes curricula and videos for men's groups as well as women's groups. The list of examples of emotional abuse is used in women's counseling.

EMOTIONAL ABUSE
- Ignored your feelings
- Ridiculed or insulted women as a group
- Ridiculed or insulted your most valued beliefs, religion, race, heritage, or class
- Withheld approval, appreciation, or affection as punishment

- Continually criticized you, called you names, shouted at you
- Humiliated you in private or public
- Threatened to hurt you or your family
- Abused, tortured, killed, or threatened to do this to your pets
- Harassed you about affairs he imagined you were having, told you about his affairs, and compared those women to you
- Destroyed furniture, punched holes in walls, broke appliances, or threatened to do any of this
- Emotionally degraded you in private, but was charming in public

APPENDIX FOUR:

WHY WOMEN DON'T LEAVE

A questionnaire to battered women to help them identify reasons why they remain in abusive relationships. It is distributed by the Duluth Domestic Abuse Intervention Project.

1. Fear of losing children.
2. Fear of physical harm.
3. Love for my partner. Wanting to be together.
4. Believed things would get better.
5. Afraid of negative impact on children.
6. Afraid of failure: family, friends, community.
7. Religious beliefs.
8. Feeling helpless, nothing will help.
9. Guilt about some of the things I've done wrong. I feel guilty, blamed myself for the violence.
10. Lack of financial resources.
11. Negative responses from community, police, courts, social workers, etc.
12. Unable to use current resources because of the way they were provided (language, disability, etc.).
13. My partner was starting to do the things I had been asking for.
14. Fear of partner doing something to get me (report me to welfare, etc.).
15. I needed time to plan and prepare to leave.

16. I thought I was too (   ) to make it on my own. (Fill in the blank: dumb, fat, ugly, or use your own words.)
17. If I stayed, I at least knew what to expect (better sense of control).
18. Fear of unknown/fear of change.
19. Fear of being without a mate/partner. This is the best I can do.
20. I wanted to keep the violence a secret from family, friends, others.
21. Exhaustion—too tired to do anything.

APPENDIX FIVE:

EARLY WARNING SIGNS FOR FUTURE ABUSE

Distibuted by the Duluth Domestic Abuse Intervention Project.

Many of the behaviors that society socializes women to interpret as caring, attentive, and romantic are actually early warning signs for future abuse.

1. Intrusion — he constantly wants to know your whereabouts, who you were with, where you were going, when you were coming home.

Examples: constant phone calls, showing up at a friend's house unexpectedly

At first this makes you feel missed and cared for, but in actuality, these are signs of his suspicion and distrust.

2. Isolation — spending all or the majority of your time alone together, cutting you off from friends and family, making fun of any activities, books, clubs you are interested in.

Examples: calling friends "sluts," "stupid," or other derogatory names, discourages you from keeping in touch with family, discourages you from doing activities apart.

This makes you feel wanted and needed because he devotes all his time to you. Actually, this cuts down on your resources (friends, family), so when you really need them, they may not be there for you.

3. Possession and Jealousy — constant accusations of sexual interactions with anyone in your life (teachers, bosses, counselors, friends, etc.), accuses you of flirting, monitoring what you wear, how you wear it, how much makeup you put on.

Examples: "I want you to be all mine," "I don't want any other guys looking at you," "You look like a whore with all that makeup on."

This is treating you like an object, not a human being.

4. Prone to Anger — easily angered, quick mood changes, unpredictable behavior, anger out of proportion to the incident.

Examples: his anger is directed toward a pet, possessions, objects — he might kick your dog, tear up some of your pictures, you show up to class five minutes late and he is overly angry.

It is important not to ignore what may seem like small overreactions. It is not acceptable for someone to use aggression to get a point across. Just because men are almost expected to be more violent, it does not mean it's OK.

5. Unknown Pasts and Respect for Women — Do you know about his past girlfriends, his family upbringing, his relationship with his mother and other women? How does he refer to women — "bitches," sex objects? Does he respect any women in his life? How do his friends look at women? Does he believe in stereotypic male/female roles?

Example: "Women are good for only one thing,"

pinching your body parts when he knows you don't like that.

It is important to take the "mystery" out of his past, by talking to his ex-girlfriends. Be in touch with your feelings — how do you feel when he degrades women? By degrading women, he is also degrading you.

Source: Browne, A. *When Battered Women Kill.* New York: The Free Press, 1987.

APPENDIX SIX:

ORGANIZATIONS AND PROGRAMS

Center for the Prevention of Sexual and Domestic
    Violence
1914 North 34th Street, Suite 105
Seattle, WA 98103
(206) 634-1903
Council for Safe Families
(914) 969-5800

Emerge
18 Hurley Street
Cambridge, MA 02141
(617) 547-9870

Family Violence Prevention Fund
1001 Potrero Avenue, Building One, Suite 200
San Francisco, CA 94110
(415) 821-4553

Family Violence and Sexual Assault Institute
1310 Clinic Drive
Tyler, TX 75701
(903) 595-6600
(903) 595-6799 fax

National Alliance on Family Violence
1155 Connecticut Avenue, N.W., Suite 300
Washington, D.C. 20036
(202) 429-6695
(800) 222-2000

National Clearinghouse for the Defense of Battered
   Women
125 South Ninth Street, Suite 302
Philadelphia, PA 19107
(215) 351-0010
(215) 351-0779 fax

National Clearinghouse on Battered Women's Self-
   Defense
524 McKnight Street
Reading, PA 19601
(215) 373-5697

National Clearinghouse on Marital and Date Rape
2325 Oak Street
Berkeley, CA 94708
(510) 524-1582

National Coalition Against Domestic Violence
P.O. Box 18749
Denver, CO 80218-0749

National Coalition of Physicians Against Family
   Violence
c/o American Medical Association
Department of Mental Health
515 North State Street
Chicago, IL 60610

National Training Project
Duluth Domestic Abuse Intervention Project
206 West Fourth Street
Duluth, MN 55806
(218) 722-2781

National Council on Child Abuse and Family Violence
1155 Connecticut Avenue, N.W., Suite 400
Washington, D.C. 20036
(202) 429-6695
(800) 222-2000

National Organization for Victim Assistance
1757 Park Road, N.W.
Washington, D.C. 20010
(800) TRY-NOVA (879-6682) Information and Referral
    Only 24 hours
(202) 232-6682 Crisis Counseling 24 hours
(202) 462-2255 Fax 24 hours

The Healing Woman
P.O. Box 3038
Moss Beach, CA 94038
(415) 728-0339

Women Against Abuse
P.O. Box 13758
Philadelphia, PA 19101
(215) 386-1280
(215) 686-7082 Legal Center
(215) 386-6312 Administrative Offices

Women Helping Women
525 North Van Buren Avenue
Stoughton, WI 53589
(608) 783-3747

SOURCE NOTES

CHAPTER ONE

1. Lawrence Sherman (Federal Bureau Of Investigation, U.S. Dept. of Justice, Washington, D.C.), "Domestic Violence," 1, Crime Files, #NCJ 97220.

2. Centers for Disease Control, "Facts on Domestic Violence," published in Legal Resource Kit, *Violence Against Women* (New York: N.O.W. Legal Defense and Education Funds, Inc., 1992), 1.

3. Sherman, 1.

CHAPTER TWO

1. Lenore Walker, *The Battered Woman* (New York: Harper & Row, 1979), 25.

2. Angela Browne, *When Battered Women Kill* (New York: Free Press, 1987), 71.

CHAPTER SIX

1. Caroline Wolf Harlow, Ph.D. *Female Victims of Violent Crime* (U.S. Dept. of Justice: Washington, D.C., 1991), 1.

2. Ibid, 1-2.

3. Victim Services Society, *Facts on Domestic Abuse* (Victim Services Society: New York, 1992), pamphlet.

CHAPTER SEVEN

1. Angela Browne, *When Battered Women Kill* (New York: Free Press, 1987), 115.
2. *Time*, January 18, 1993, 45.

CHAPTER EIGHT

1. Angela Browne, *When Battered Women Kill* (New York: Free Press, 1987), 21.
2. *Time*, "Do Us Part," Nancy Gibbs, January 18, 1993, 45.
3. Browne, 20.
4. Ibid, 3.
5. Ibid, 71.
6. Time, 45.
7. Ibid, 45-48.
8. National Institute of Justice, *Civil Protection Orders: A Unique Opportunity for Court Intervention* (Washington, D.C.: National Institute of Justice, 1990), 1.
9. Del Martin, *Battered Wives* (New York: Pocket Books, 1983), 33.
10. Susan Steinmets and Murray Straus, eds., *Violence in the Family* (New York: Dodd, Mead, 1975), Robert Calvert, "Criminal and Civil Liability in Husband–Wife Assaults," 88, 89.

CHAPTER NINE

1. Del Martin, *Battered Wives* (New York: Pocket Books, 1983), 198.
2. Personal conversations with battered women.

BIBLIOGRAPHY

Ammerman, R. T., and M. Herson, eds. *Treatment of Family Violence: A Sourcebook*. New York: John Wiley, 1990.

Buzawa, E., and C. Buzawa. *Domestic Violence: The Criminal Justice Response*. Newbury Park, Calif.: Sage Publications, Inc., 1990.

Carmody, D. C., and K. R. Williams. "Wife assault and perceptions of sanctions." *Violence and Victims*, 2 (1): 25–39, 1987.

Costa, J. *Abuse of Women: Legislation, Reporting, and Prevention*. Lexington, Mass.: D. C. Heath and Company, 1983.

Dobash, R. E., and R. Dobash. *Violence Against Wives: A Case Against the Patriarchy*. New York: Free Press, 1979.

Dolon, R., J. Hendricks, and M. S. Meagher. "Police practices and attitudes toward domestic violence." *Journal of Police Science and Administration*, 14 (3), 187–192, 1986.

Dutton, D. The Domestic Assault of Women: Psychological and Criminal Justice Perspectives. Boston: Allyn and Bacon, 1988.

Ellis, J. W. "Prosecutorial discretion to charge in cases of spousal assault: A dialogue." *Journal of*

Criminal Law and Criminology, 75 (Spring), 56–102, 1984.

Fedders, C., and L. Elliot. *Shattered Dreams.* New York: Harper and Row Publishers, 1987.

Finkelhor, D., R. Gelles, G. Hotaling, and M. Straus, eds. *The Dark Side of Families.* Newbury Park, Calif.: Sage Publications, Inc., 1983.

Gandolf, E. *Men Who Batter: An Integrated Approach for Stopping Wife Abuse.* Holmes Beach, Fla.: Learning Publications, Inc., 1985.

Gelles, R., and M. Straus. *Intimate Violence.* New York: Simon and Schuster, 1988.

Goolkasian, G. A. "The judicial system and domestic violence: An expanding role." *Response.* 9 (4), 2–7, 1986.

Hanmer, J., J. Radford, and E. Stanko, eds. *Women, policing and male violence: International perspectives.* London: Routledge and Keegan Paul, 1989.

Hart, W., J. Ashcroft, A. Burgess, N. Flanagan, C. Meese, C. Milton, C. Narramores, R. Oretega, and F. Seward. *Attorney General's Task Force on Family Violence.* Washington, D.C.: Government Printing Office, 1984.

Lerman, L. "Mediation of Wife Abuse Cases: The Adverse Impact of Informal Dispute Resolution of Women." *Harvard Women's Law Journal,* 7, 65–67, 1984.

Levinson, D. *Family Violence in a Cross Cultural Perspective.* Newbury Park, Calif.: Sage Publications, 1989.

Loving, N. *Spouse Abuse: A Curriculum Guide for Police Trainers.* Police Executive Research Forum, 1981.

NiCarthy, G. *The Ones Who Got Away: Women Who Left Abusive Partners.* Seattle, Washington: Seal Press, 1987.

Ohlin, L., and M. Tonry, eds. *Family Violence.* Chicago: University of Chicago Press, 1989.

Pagelow, M. *Family Violence.* New York: Praeger Publishers, 1984.

Pahl, J., ed. *Private Violence and Public Policy.* Boston, Mass.: Routledge and Kegan Paul, 1985.

Rouse, L. *You Are Not Alone: A Guide for Battered Women.* Holmes Beach, Fla.: Learning Publications, Inc., 1986.

Schechter, S. *Women and Male Violence.* Boston, Mass.: South End Press, 1982.

Schmidt, J., and E. H. Steury. "Prosecutorial discretion in filing charges in domestic violence cases." *Criminology* 27 (3), 487–510, 1984.

Sonkin, D. J., D. Martin, and L. E. Walker, eds. *Male Batterer.* New York: Springer, 1985.

Straus, M. A., and G. T. Hotaling, eds. *Social Causes of Husband/Wife Violence.* Minneapolis: University of Minnesota Press, 1980.

Victim Services Agency. *The Law Enforcement Response to Domestic Violence.* (Manual). New York: Victim Services Agency, 1988.

Walker, L. D., ed. *The Battered Woman Syndrome.* New York: Springer Publishing, 1984.

Wilt, M., and J. Bannon. *Domestic Violence and the Police: Studies in Detroit and Kansas City.* Washington, D.C.: The Police Foundation, 1977.

Yilo, M., and M. Bograd, eds. *Feminist Perspectives on Wife Abuse.* Newbury Park, Calif.: Sage Publications, 1988.

INDEX

ABOUT THE AUTHOR

ANNA KOSOF, a producer of television and radio documentaries, and the former general manager of radio station WBGO-FM in Newark, New Jersey, recently coproduced the "Gorbachev Project" for public broadcasting. Her most recent book for Franklin Watts is *The Civil Rights Movement and Its Legacy*.